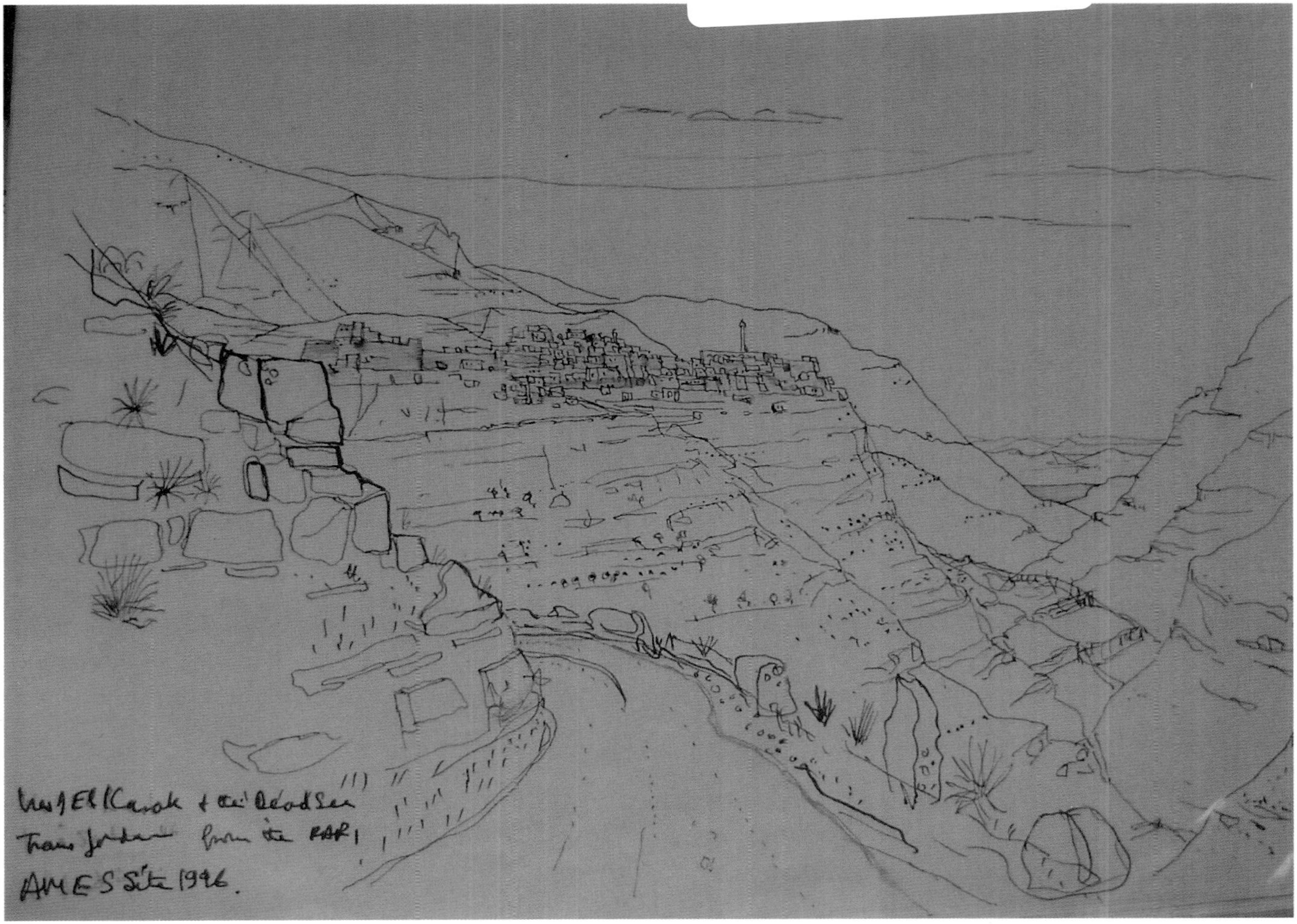

Wady El Karak & the Dead Sea
Trans Jordan from the RAF,
AMES Site 1946.

Beneath the Radar

Beneath the Radar

An illustrated account of an ordinary radar operator's life in RAF Radar Stations 1942-6

Nina Baker

Copyright © 2021 Nina Baker
All rights reserved. This book or any portion thereof may not be reproduced or used in any manner whatsoever without the express written permission of the publisher except for the use of brief quotations in a book review or scholarly journal. Please note that I control copyright over all the original artwork, so contact me if you have any wish to use any of it: nina.baker1@btinternet.com
First Printing: 2021

Crampton-Moorhouse Publishing
Glasgow, Scotland
ISBN: 9798471940635

In memory of my father, Ian Baker, who is missed every day.

Contents

Epilogue 9
How To Build A Radar Operator 15
Billets and Transfer Camps 36
AMES, RADAR and MRUs 40
The Last Troopship Voyage of the Felix Roussel 43
    The Story Of The Ship 43
    Life on board the troopship 46
    The Voyage 61
Palestine, Jordan, Egypt and Libya 71
    Life in camp 80
    Palestine 94
    Libya 98
        GEE 101
        Garian 104
        The road to demob 137
Prelude to another life 143
Acknowledgements 144
Bibliography 145

Epilogue

My father, Ian Baker, died on 11 May 2010. I suppose it is a commonplace truism that children often come to know their parents' lives in more detail after they have died – when papers, diaries and friends' memories come to light in the aftermath. I had always known in a vague way that my father's Royal Air Force service had had a connection with radar, but neither he nor my mother could be persuaded to talk about the war to any extent. From many emerging personal histories of the Second World War, and indeed its dreadful predecessor, The Great War, it is apparent that many, if not most, people chose not to speak of their experiences, whether relatively benign or appalling, top secret or mundane.

When I was very small, I had their service medals and WAAF/RAF sleeve badges to play with, but my parents cared nothing for these mementos and they have somehow become lost along the way. It was only at the very end of his life and after his death I realised there might be enough to make an interesting story, and by then he was gone, my mother was also long gone and there was no one else left to ask. So, this book is based on the physical materials I still have, supported by conventional archive research to fill in some gaps.

This book has been assembled from three key types of materials, which came into my hands when my father died: photos and negatives; drawings and paintings; and handwritten letters to my mother, Patricia Rawlinson. The photos and the negatives I had more or less always known about because my father introduced me to the basics of enlarging and printing photos in a makeshift darkroom at home when I was little, in the 1960s. Some of the photos in my possession are enlargements done then. A few others I have used in this book were small prints for which no negatives are to hand. Of his fat little negative storage album, only a tiny proportion show anything pertinent to the subject of this account.

By chance, the Royal Institute of British Architects (RIBA) had commissioned a series of monographs about mid-twentieth century architectural practices and my father's firm, Leonard Manasseh & Partners, was selected as one of those to be written about. A leading architectural history academic, Tim Brittain-Caitlin, was asked to write the book[1] and first contacted me about this in 2009. We discussed what I could personally recollect of the history of the firm and he also interviewed my father twice, although my father's powers of recall were fading fast by then. However, the book for the RIBA would have to have illustrations so I set about hunting through my father's London house for what there might still be left. Unfortunately, many of the sketches, paintings and plans of the firm's work over the years had been lost or destroyed, so it was a question of finding what little might remain.

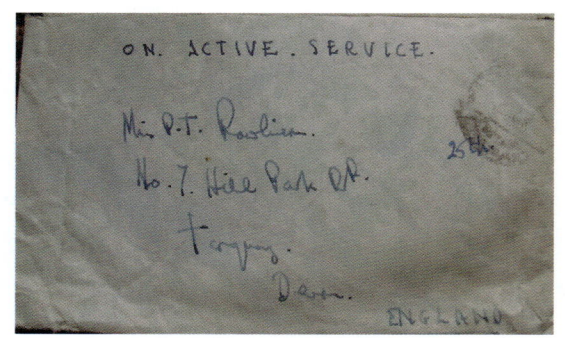

---
[1] Leonard Manasseh & Partners. Tim Brittain-Caitlin. RIBA Publishing. 2011. ISBN9781859463680

Bearing in mind that my father's large house in south London was where I had lived with my parents for a few years as an adult before leaving home and that I had myself stored stuff in the attic, I thought I knew pretty much what there was, but I was wrong. In pulling portfolios and drawing-tubes and fat brown paper packages down out of the loft, poking around in sketch books and drawers full of this and that, I was surprised by what came to light. Sifting through to find what Tim needed, I also ended up with another pile of no particular interest to his book but which makes the backbone to this one you are holding. These were a sketch book plus many loose pages of pen and ink sketches and ink wash paintings, of scenes from my father's travels with the RAF. In some cases, they are essentially corroborative evidence filling in the gaps left by what the far smaller number of photographs can tell us.

I also found a package of letters that my father wrote to my mother during 1945-6. I cannot now recall if I retrieved these when my mother died the mid-1990s, or if my father had hung on to them after they divorced in the early 1970s and they had somehow just never been disposed of. These are, sadly, only one side of the conversation as I have nothing at all written by my mother in that period. It is evident that my father was head over heels in love at the time and the letters are very affectionate.
They seem to have been written at close intervals although not all are dated. My father's handwriting was always dire and takes a bit of getting used to, even once past barriers of the fading ink or pencil on poor quality wartime paper. Naturally, they do not refer to technical matters as presumably his work would have been considered to be secret, even though most of the letters were written after the end of the actual war.

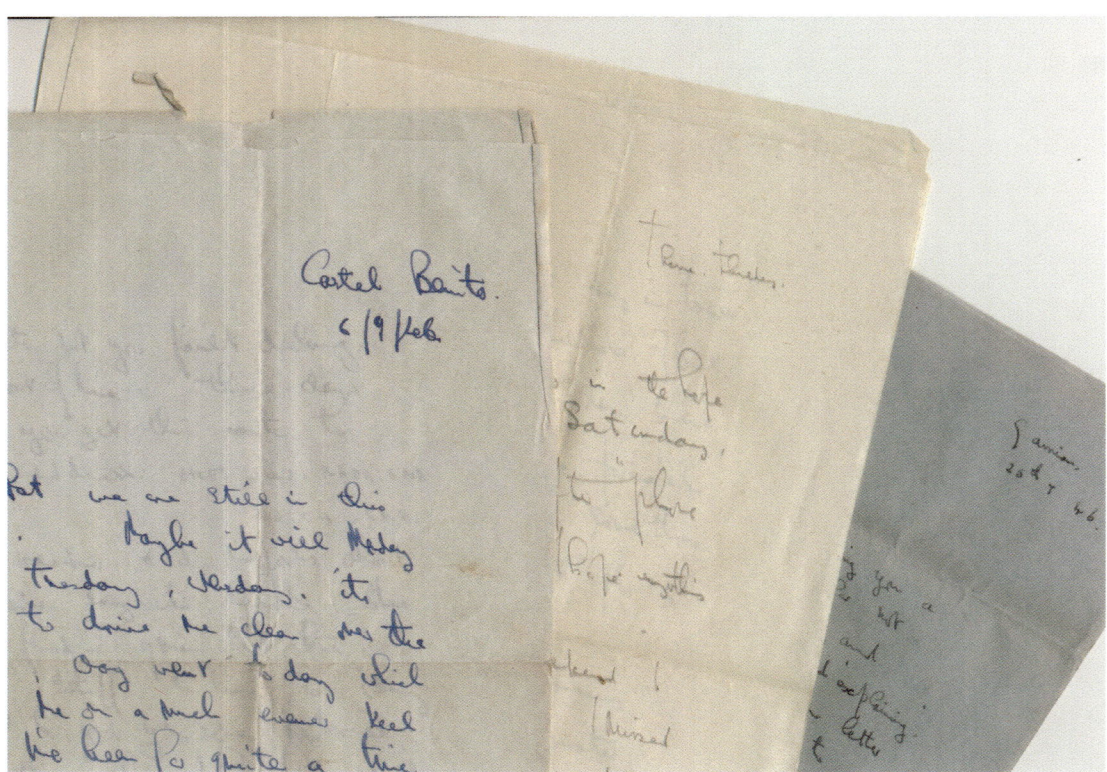

Together they make what I think may be a unique picture of a particular corner of the history of early radar: the MRUs and AMES[2] establishments in the Middle East at the end of the war. There are many books and websites devoted to radar's history and place in the winning of the war, and the high-profile 'boffins' who developed it, but I have found much less on the particular types and locations of equipment that my father worked on, let alone the ordinary operators. This is why I thought this might be worth writing.

---

[2] MRU was originally the acronym for Mobile Radio Unit but in post-war usage it has come to mean Mobile Radar Unit. AMES, acronym for Air Ministry Experimental Station, meaning radar's birthplace at Bawdsey Research Station (BRS), but later the acronym for all RAF radar stations.

This book, presented in an informal style, not intended to be an academic history but does include some references for those who might be interested to know more. It is presented in sections covering Ian's training and time in the UK before being sent abroad, his time on the troopship, the equipment he worked with and finally his time in the Middle East and North Africa prior to demobilisation. By the time he was sent abroad, the war in Europe was over and he never saw any combat action.

You can read delightful and affectionate obituaries of my father in The Times, The Guardian or the Architects' Journal but they predominantly deal with his professional life as a successful architect after his war service. The account that follows relates to the period of a young man growing up in strange locations and under uncomfortable circumstances. My father was insignificant in the great scheme of the War and the history of radar, but his drawings and paintings add, I think, a unique flavour to the history of that period, from the standpoint of a very ordinary young man, from literally and metaphorically 'beneath the radar'.

Top: preparing for one of Mill Hill School's famous roller-skate pageants, perhaps around 1936. Ian is the 'knight' top left.

Left: Mill Hill School building.

How To Build A Radar Operator

Ian was only a schoolboy of 16, as a boarding pupil at Mill Hill School, when the Second World War broke out in 1939. His school was evacuated, from North London to the Lake District for his final year of schooling. He left school at 17, without achieving any qualifications, having shown no academic aptitude for anything except art and long-distance running.

Following a year (1940-41) at the University of Aberystwyth getting a diploma in art, his taciturn father perceived that Ian might become an architect and found an art tutor to help him prepare the necessary portfolio to apply to an architectural school. Bearing in mind that my father had so far failed every available scholastic exam, and would probably nowadays have been considered to have both dyslexia and dyscalculia, this was quite a hurdle even in those less formal times. Other applicants would have had not only substantial portfolios of artwork but also the 'matriculation' certificates required to enter university. Matriculation, as it was known, taken about age 18, was the then equivalent of A-levels, with the lower 'School cert' taken 2 years before that, being similar to GSCEs. He had none of that and used to say that to get an idea of his school life, the Billy Bunter books about boys in the 'remove' classes were about right.

Sketch of a house in Aberystwyth.

The art tutor must also have been able to discern the potential that Ian had within him and started him off with the biggest piece of paper my father had ever seen. Since this was presumably on a drawing board, we can assume this was probably similar to an A0 sheet of today. On this one piece of paper did my father's whole professional future depend as this was to become a 'measured drawing' of St Paul's Cathedral in London.

The measured drawing is an exercise that students of architecture have to master in order to understand how drawings relate to three dimensional actual buildings. The key text book for this, of that period and which is still in print today, was "Architectural Drawing" by Richard Phene Spiers, a distant ancestor on his mother's side. His copy of this book is still in the family and shows clear signs of intensive use. This massive drawing, when completed, was to constitute Ian's sole evidence on applying to architectural school: no Higher School Certificate passes, no portfolio, just a single roll of paper. It seems that the AA school had some discretion to waive the normal academic requirements and he was duly admitted to the Architectural Association's school in 1941-2.

In late 1941, at just 18 years of age, he was called up for war service into the RAF and attended the Air Crew Selection Board (ACSB) No.11 on 8th December, at the Combined Recruiting Centre, where recruits for all three services reported on call-up. Having passed the ACSB with a classification for observer training, he was then enlisted on 8th January 1942 and passed along to the 1 ACRC (Air Crew Reception Centre) as part of the Euston Reserve.

The selection process at this time was pretty elementary[3]. Prior to 1940, the RAF selected new recruits for air crew and commissions by means of an unstructured interview conducted by serving officers who were essentially looking for the right 'types'. There were no formal criteria as to personality, attainment, aptitude or skills. Clearly the process was a uniformed version of the classic and class-obsessed British 'Old Boy network' – if a man had been to the 'right school', was reasonably well turned-out and sporty, he was probably recommended for a commission and if he could ride too then he probably had the coordination and courage for pilot training.

However, the failure rate from this informal process was appalling: about 50% sent for aircrew training failed (or worse, crashed fatally) in the early part of their training. The first changes to be brought in, devised by Prof. F.C. Bartlett of Cambridge University for the RAF, in an effort to introduce some semblance of a system, were essay writing, an Elementary Maths Test and a General Intelligence Test. These became the first objective 'aircrew selection test battery' and had 5 lettered grades, although no pass/fail cut-off point was initially set.

By 1941, the RAF had its own centralised research unit, the Training Research Branch, which developed aptitude tests, selection methods and training programmes. This unit soon recognised the need to assess for personality characteristics as well as skills. In 1942, a Flying Grading process was introduced which entailed a short period of 12 hours flying at an Elementary Flying Training school in which the students' performance was recorded, assessed and analysed. In 1942 a

---

[3]Evolution Of Aptitude Testing In The RAF. M. Bailey. Paper presented at the RTO HFM Workshop on "Officer Selection" held in Monterey, USA, 9-11 November 1999, and published in RTO MP-55.

further set of preliminary practical tests was devised to select pilots and wireless operators, which led to further reductions in wastage on aircrew training courses.

By the end of the war, these tests had developed to such a degree that there was a total of 24 tests to select for all the 6 aircrew specialisations. One of the new trade specialisms offered to women entering the WAAF, when it expanded beyond the clerical and catering fields, was as psychology assistants running these batteries of tests for new entrants to the RAF and WAAF. There is a Pathé newsreel[4] of the type of aptitude tests that were in use immediately after the war (1949), some of which were probably very similar to those introduced in 1942. The simulated radar screen activity bears a striking resemblance to simple computer games familiar to our own era.

The ACSB in 1941 recommended Ian for a commission, and aircrew training as an observer, but this was deferred, for him to continue his architectural studies, as the rules allowed students to defer their normal call-up for their first year of undergraduate studies. During this period, it is likely that he applied to the London Joint Universities Recruitment Board (JURB), which was open to any undergraduate to seek a commission in any of the three services. Certainly, there seems to have been no other explicit selection process mentioned in his service records, for a commission. His records do however show that he was a member of the London University Air Squadron although what training he might have received is not apparent. The JURBs must have been outside the call-up process as there is no mention on my father's service record relating to it.

---

[4] RAF Aptitude Tests Film ID: 1369.16 https://www.britishpathe.com/video/raf-aptitude-tests/query/wildcard

Interior design sketch, from Ian's sketch book which he carried with him in his Middle East tour of duty.

Consequently, he spent the academic year of 1941-42 at the Architectural Association (AA), probably at its evacuation premises in Hendon, rather than its home in Bedford Square in the West End of London. His records show that he got outstanding results in all his assessments, achieving increasing numbers of merit and merit-exhibition grades. He tried to fit in as much architectural education as he could and took an extra term over what would otherwise have been the summer vacation of 1942 and even continuing into the first term of his second year, in 1942-43 right up until the point when he had to actually go off for RAF training. Throughout his war service he took his drawing kit with him and kept in touch with AA friends when he could, although he often mentions the difficulty of getting hold of paper to draw on. A drawing board, set square and T-square, even small ones, must have been terribly awkward to lug around in a military environment where all your kit was meant to fit into a cylindrical canvas kit bag, but he took them even when sent overseas.

In early 1943 he was finally ordered to report for duty. Although he started the course at Number 1 Air Crew Reception Centre (ACRC, Babbacombe, near Torquay in Devon) in March 1943, and then at 11 Initial Training Wing (11 ITW) in Scarborough, something must have proved beyond him as, in May, he had been withdrawn and sent back to SHQ for assessment and re-grading to ACH u/t RDF/Op (The RAF's long-winded acronym for an Aircraft Hand Radio Direction Finder Operator under training). In these early days of radar technology, the Services continued the fiction that radar was only the basic direction finding from radio beacons, hence the trade was known RDF Operator, although it was later on changed to Radar Operator. The female equivalent in the WAAFs were known as Clerks (Special Duties).

It is not clear where his basic training would have been, but there is a short newsreel clip of some aspects of initial training RAF-style on the Pathé website. He did mention doing freezing runs during training at St Andrews in Scotland, but there is nowhere mentioned in his service records that would tally with this, and I think he may have confused St Andrews with Scarborough, also a coastal town subject to the same biting east coast winds. He was a reasonably fit young man although not sturdily built, being beanpole thin into middle age, and I would think the running parts of basic training would have been easier for him than carrying heavy packs and so on.

In some ways I am amazed he was ever considered for aircrew, or even radar work as I would have thought both would have required reasonable maths which he certainly did not have. Perhaps his

initial assessment at the ACSB was still heavily influenced by the fact that he had been to a public school and was a prize-winning cross-country runner and they chose to ignore his utter absence of academic qualifications in the light of the time he had just spent at university. Throughout his adult life he always used mechanical and, latterly, digital calculators for any arithmetical calculations (bending moments in structures for example). An attempt to train him as a radar mechanic seems to have fallen foul of the same problem, although he was always a practical person, but presumably his innate sense of two dimensional and three-dimensional spaces that would be the bedrock of his architectural career, was ideal for work as a radar operator. It is not clear whether his early RAF service, post-training, was as a radar operator in the sense of the plotters or spotters who watched the screens for incoming ships or aircraft.

In June 1943 he was at he was sent to RAF Sutton Coldfield (216 Maintenance Unit), probably just as a 'holding' posting, leaving there 4 August 1943. He then went to RAF Yatesbury, the location of the main radar operators' training school: No 9 Radio School (5 August 1943 – 22 September 1943). One of the radar instructors at that time was a newly commissioned Pilot Officer (Technical Branch), Arthur C Clarke, who went on to become the famous scientist and science-fiction author. Clarke had a reputation as an inspiring instructor. No 9 Radio School was a massive establishment where both ground-based and airborne radar operators were trained together. The chief instructing officer for most of the war at Yatesbury was Squadron Leader Danielson.[5]

Amongst the skills that the first Chain Home Low (CHL) radar operators had had to master were the combined hand-eye-foot actions required to keep the transmitter (Tx) and receiver (Rx) pointing in the same

---

[5] Radar a wartime miracle. C. Latham & A. Stobbs, Sutton Publishing Ltd, 1996.

direction, by means of a centre-zero voltmeter whilst also rotating the aerials by means of pedals connected to a 'Heath Robinson' type arrangement of cranks and chains. However, by 1943, things had changed considerably with the hand-cranked CHL system replaced almost everywhere with a more robust system of combined single aerials. Despite the thousands of ground and aircrew being trained in radar here and elsewhere (including in Canada) the utmost secrecy was the strict rule. In the earliest days the WAAFs and RAF men were not even allowed to take notes back to their billets or barracks. It must have been very difficult to learn this very new material without the chance to revise in the evenings from your notes. Such notebooks were regarded as Secret documents which could only follow the trainee to subsequent postings if sent in the Classified mail by the Signals Wing.

The training must have been very intensive because within 6 weeks, Ian was apparently considered to be sufficiently trained. This seems to have been typical as other personal histories of radar operators often report only 3 weeks training in the early days. The six weeks training course for operators included a detachment period of 'on the job' training. He was sent to 78 Wing on 23 September 1943. The HQ for 78 Wing was at RAF Ashburton in Devon and the wing controlled many radar stations. Unfortunately, his service record is not very specific at this point, so it is not possible to know exactly which radar stations he was at. Certainly, it seems he must have met my mother, who was a WAAF Radar Plotter when they were both stationed in Devon, probably at or near Kingswear in 1943. RAF Kingswear was a Chain Home Low radar site at Coleton Camp near Coleton Fishacre, east of Kingswear, using Type 52 and 41 Radars. A mention in a later letter refers back to this time as when they were both involved in providing radar cover for shipping. This fits with these radar types, since Type 41 sets were variants of low and medium power systems based on the naval 10cm wavelength equipment and were used for 'coastwatching' duties. Type 52 systems were higher powered 10cm wavelength, machines, again based on naval radar, and had circular parabolic aerials fixed on a gantry above the operating hut. During his time in Devon Ian was promoted to AC1 and then to Leading Aircraftman.

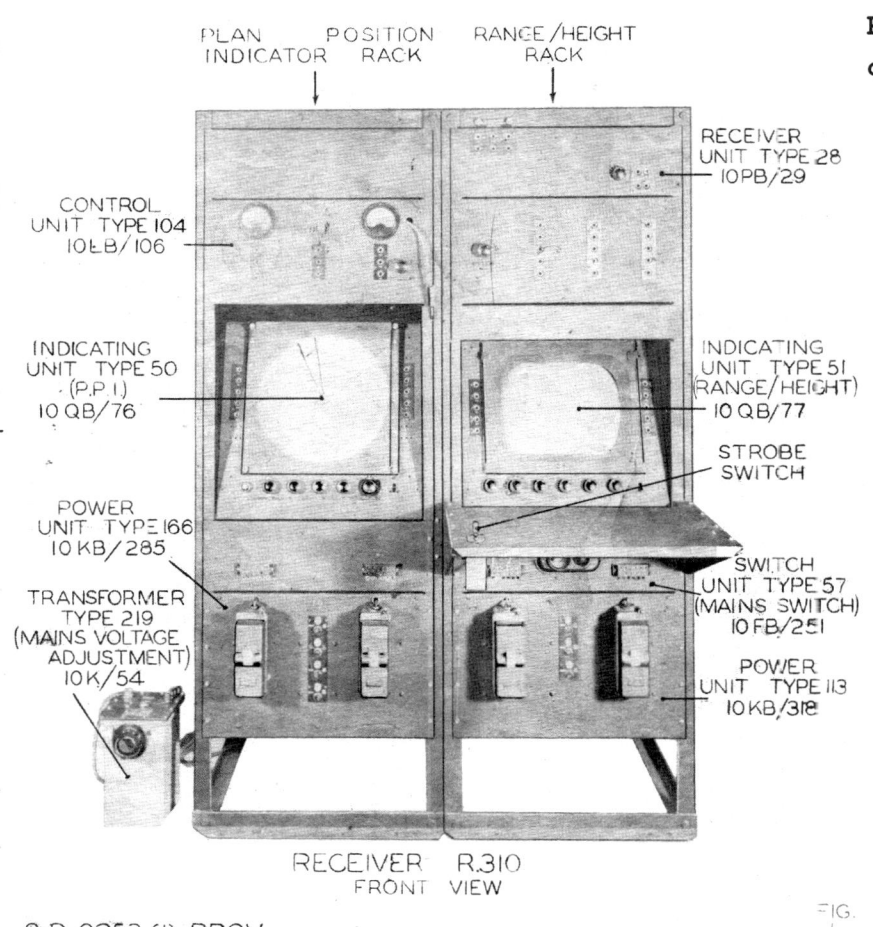

Radar set lay-out (Image courtesy of Mike Dean)

Ian never seemed to linger long at any one RAF station and his time in Devon came to an end in November 1944 when he was sent to 73 Wing, in Yorkshire, which was responsible for the ground radar units from the River Tees to the Wash. Again, it is unclear which particular stations he might have been working at but in March 1945 he was, for some reason, assessed for and then rejected from training as a radar mechanic, no great surprise given his lack of maths. Then from 11 May to 5 June 1945 he was back down south again, at the Chain Home station at Worth Matravers, also known as Renscombe Down, near Swanscombe in Dorset.

At some point around this time, he must have had retraining, as the machinery he was to operate when he was sent oversees was the GEE radar navigation system.

Albert Grieveson's story[6] of his time as a radar operator suggests that Renscombe was at this time acting as an assembly line for people being pulled together into groups to make up small mobile radar units (MRUs), known as AMES type 14s.

This is confirmed by Mick Miller's story[7] of his time there, in which he describes Renscombe as a place where mobile radar crews received what almost amounted to commando training prior to being shipped abroad. Miller was being prepared for active service during the post-D-Day expeditions in Europe and Africa, which would not have been the case by the time my father was at Renscombe. However, everyone there was rigorously drilled in how to erect the various types of mast

---

[6] Wanderings of a Radar Operator by BBC Radio Norfolk Action Desk
https://www.bbc.co.uk/history/ww2peopleswar/stories/29/a4492929.shtml

[7] Radar a wartime miracle. C. Latham & A. Stobbs, Sutton Publishing Ltd, 1996.

frameworks that came either in a nested set of box frames or as a set of Meccano-style beams and trusses to be bolted together. Miller recalled:

> "At Renscombe I became part of a mobile radar unit called a type 14. There were eighteen or nineteen of us including the CO, pilot officer, cook, driver, nursing orderly, mechanics and general duties."

Life at Renscombe might have been less than great, as my father contrived to lose a day's seniority there, presumably due to some minor misdemeanour – getting drunk perchance? In less than a month Ian had been sent to RAF Thame, which housed an Overseas Packing Unit and was near Haddenham, Buckinghamshire. The unit was responsible for crating up equipment for shipping overseas use by the RAF. Most of the work was the dispatching of radar and radio navigation beacons, which finished in April 1946. The awfulness of Haddenham was notorious and no respecter of rank, service or even nationality. RAF Thame was infamous for its boredom and the high risk of infection from the water, perhaps the masses of troops encamped there had not been adequately provided for in the way of sewerage. An American woman pilot working with the Air Transport Auxiliary reported that everyone was ill all the time there[8].

---

[8] Jane Spencer quoted at http://www.haddenhamairfieldhistory.co.uk/ferrypilots.htm

Another RAF serviceman[9] described it as:

"… nothing but a vast expanse of tents, even the cook-house was a marquee. So many tents in fact that he didn't even realise he was on an airfield. He recalls that the whole place was terrible especially the state of the water and his abiding thought of Haddenham is that he should have been inoculated before arriving!"

[9] Ken Harrup quoted at http://www.haddenhamairfieldhistory.co.uk/closingdown.htm

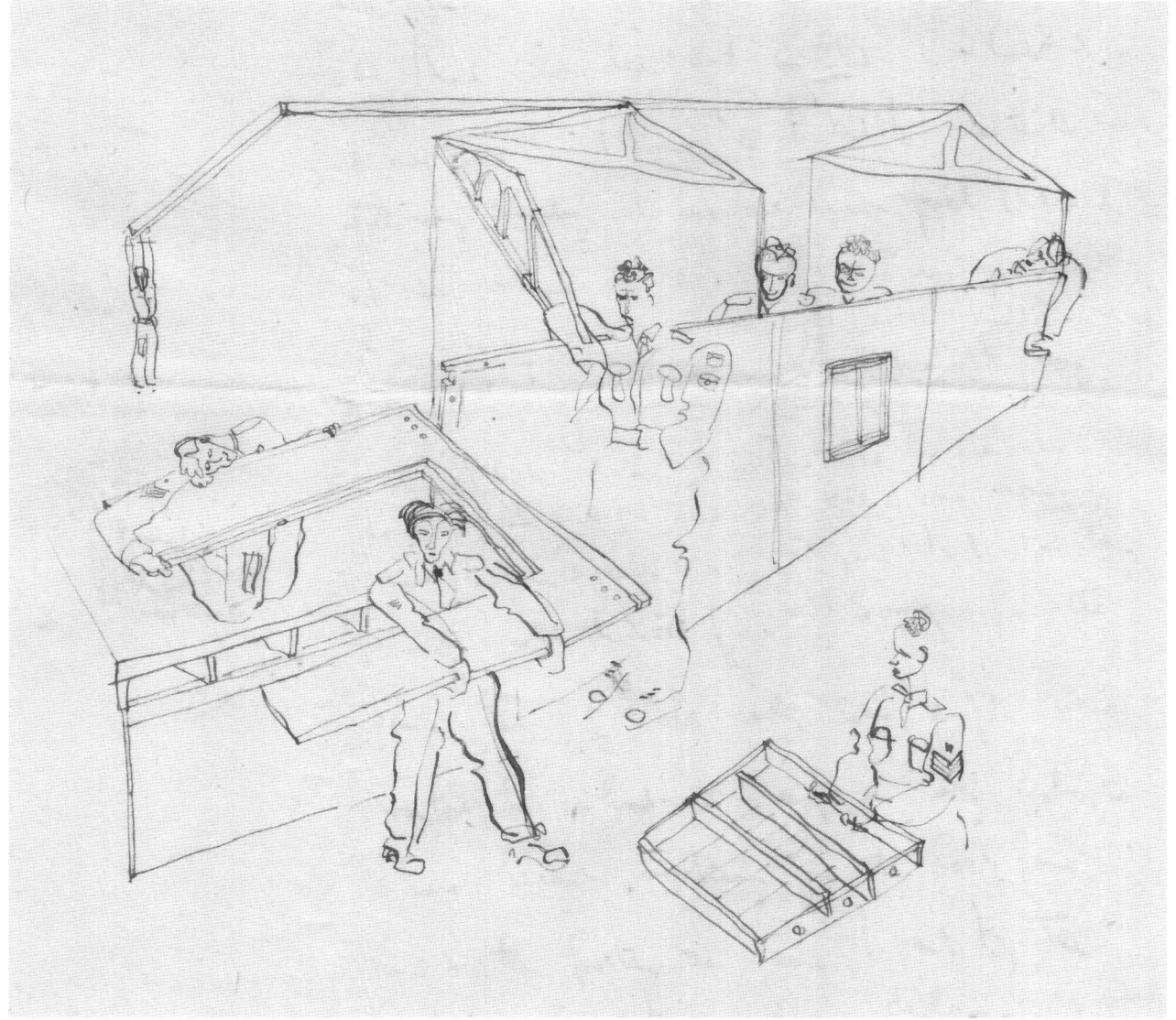

Cartoon of Ian's unit under training in putting up flat-packed huts, RAF Thame.

This is the first point at which I have letters sent to my mother, Patricia, by my father, possibly because they had previously been stationed at RAF units near each other, or at least within visiting or phoning distance and this was the beginning of a period when they knew he was going to be going abroad for an unknown length of time. The first letter has an elaborately decorated cover sheet, followed by the faint pencil scrawls that passed for my father's appalling handwriting. This letter is only dated "Thursday" which is probably 7th June 1945, the day after he arrived at the RAF station. The letter is full of arrangements for a weekend leave together and depressed descriptions of a trip he had made to 'town' (London), which was very hot and full of:

> "…millions of foul people there seem to be in London these days roaming about with no particular aim in life except to see something unusual happen or pay 7/6 for a meal."

He walked around a lot, bought some art prints and visited his architect friend, 'Beak' Adams, who had been in his class at the Architectural Association School. He apparently saved money on overnight accommodation by staying in Gower Street – apparently in Beak's billet – where Ian felt it worth mentioning cooking two sausages and a pie for his dinner. 'Beak' Adams would remain a lifelong friend.

Inside a hut at RAF Thame. The writing says "This is a horrible mistake not meant to be looked at. For John's benefit"

Beneath the Radar

Being able to get to London easily must have been one of the few consolations to those stationed at RAF Thame. Ian reports that:

> "The last weekend of every month is a passless one! Which is a bit of an antiflamminagastra[10] so to speak as it means we only get Sunday off but I don't think it will effect me much as I can freelance myself at will without much bother."

This seems to imply that it was possible to come and go at RAF Thame without much supervision and another partial letter implies something similar.

The other letter from RAF Thame is not dated at all but refers to the weather being very cold and wet, so it is probably from the end of his time there – he arrived at his next posting on 5th December 1945. He was awaiting information about the next move, to go abroad. Some other groups that had been leaving there, for the Middle East, had flown instead of going by ship. His group had been engaged in learning to put up pre-fabricated huts and was called away on parade in the middle of writing the letter to be detailed off to unload a consignment of further huts.

---

[10] I think this extraordinary word must have been his own invention or a private joke with Pat, as I have not been able to find any use of it elsewhere.

He had evidently just come back from a weekend leave with Patricia and they were planning to go on another soon, in Bath, where he hoped to get himself new paintbrushes. Apparently, these were to replace some lost in a "great fire" which he apologises for even mentioning, so we don't know anything about the circumstances. This letter contains the first reference to an RAF colleague with whom he would spend most of the rest of his time in the service, referred to here as "…my Oag friend…", who is mentioned in another letter as having been a bank clerk in civvy life.

The weather was so cold and wet and the huts so chilly, being more or less glorified packing crates with 3 tier bunks, that he went to the NAAFI to hear an ENSA concert with 16 acts, not usually his sort of thing, but anything was worth it to be warm. On the back of a humorous cartoon of his squad erecting huts, is a postscript mentioning a breakfast of Spam and tomatoes as a meal of which Pat might be jealous.

Billets and Transfer Camps

RAF Thame was a staging post for mobile groups going abroad, so the next moves took Ian to billets in Blackpool whilst nominally at Number 2 Personnel Dispatch Centre (2PDC) at Kirkham in the Morecambe area. No letters survive of this highly transitory period but there are some sketches showing how very spartan these billets were, presumably in private homes or small guest houses. From these temporary lodgings they were soon embarked on board a troopship, the Felix Roussel, to be shipped to the Middle East to begin the work for which they had been selected and retrained: setting up and operating radar navigation stations.

Billet: note how the householder has crammed in 2 beds and a folding camp-bed, plus no floor coverings or lampshade.

Sketches at the billet in Morecambe 1945.

AMES, RADAR and MRUs

The Second World War saw an explosion of acronyms across every area of military and civilian life, from the affectionate SWALK[11]s on the backs of envelopes, to the rude SNAFUs of everyday military foul-ups. Many were not so much euphemisms as the means to keep secrets. Radar itself is an acronym for RAdio **D**irection **A**nd **R**anging and is the Americans' term for what started in the UK as the much less obvious RDF, or Radio Direction Finding. This latter was deliberately chosen to be the same as the navigation aid of the same name which had been in use for many years and which relied on a simple radio receiver with a rotating aerial which allowed the navigator to take a compass bearing on the strongest single from a known location of charted radio beacons. Radar operators were initially known as RDF operators in the RAF or Clerks (Special Duties) in the WAAF.

As the majority of the research that ultimately led to the successful development of radar for detecting and tracking aircraft was done with the RAF, much of the pre-war work was sponsored by the UK government's Air Ministry and both the locations of research laboratories or operating stations and also the multiplicity of machinery types were known as Air Ministry Experimental Stations or AMES, followed by a number. I found this initially very confusing as the novice researcher in this field has to grasp that a reference to an AMES might refer to a unit's location or a machine type. To further add to the confusion, AMES units in Britain were sometimes moved from place to place but worse yet, after D-Day there were many mobile AMES units that were on the move all the time and were sometimes listed interchangeably as AMES

---

[11]SWALK = Sealed with a loving kiss. SNAFU = Situation normal, all fouled up (ruder versions too!)

or MRUs (mobile radio units). Another snag for the unwary is that radar was used to refer not only to the systems for detecting and tracking aircraft and ships but also to the various navigational systems which were a further essential offshoot of the technology. There was no difference in the RAF trade titles and servicemen and women were expected to pick up the necessary expertise on the different systems very quickly. Even the radar mechanics, the elite of the RAF groundcrew trades, would often find themselves posted to a new station with no knowledge of what machinery to expect let alone any prior training.

Inside the operating cabin of a Type 14 radar unit. [Ian Baker]

View forwards from boat deck on the Felix Roussel {Ian Baker]

The Last Troopship Voyage of the Felix Roussel

The Story Of The Ship

The Felix Roussel was built for the Messageries Maritimes by Ateliers et Chantiers de la Loire, St Nazaire in 1929 and started her Far East service in 1931. She underwent several modifications during her lifetime, the first being in 1935 when she was lengthened and her engines improved to give a top speed of 13.5 knots. She continued as a liner ('paquebot') until, on a return sailing from Shanghai, the ship was detained by the British at Port Said in June 1940 and requisitioned for use in the Allied war effort.[12] Operating under the Free French flag and managed by the Bibby Line the ship received some armament and was manned by a mostly French volunteer crew.

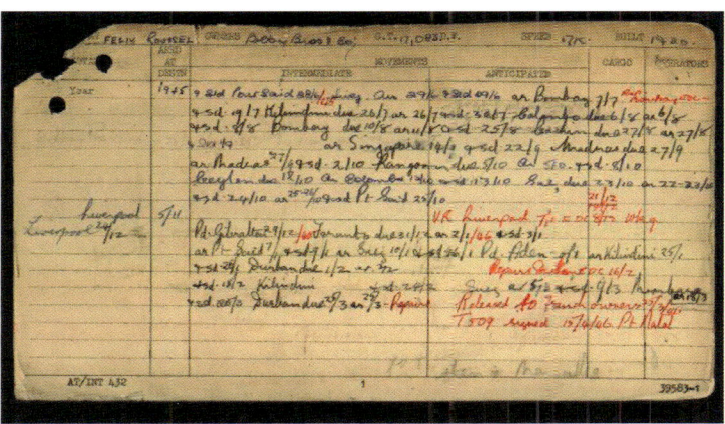

---

[12] This information largely derived from the Ministry of Shipping record card (The National Archives (Catalogue Reference: BT/389/12) and http://www.derbysulzers.com/shipfelix.html

In February 1942 the Felix Roussel was part of the last convoy to reach Singapore as it fell to the Japanese. She sustained several bomb hits, one penetrated the decks close by the bridge, another near a funnel hit a gun position killing a number of army gunners. The rudder was also damaged, but she reached the port of Singapore to discharge the troops and other cargo. She then carried at least 1,100 evacuated women and children, RAF personnel and some survivors from the Prince of Wales & Repulse, passing through the Sunda Strait under escort. On May 27th 1942 the Felix Roussel was named to the order of the Free French Forces and ten crew members received the Croix de Guerre. Captain Snowling added a bar to his Distinguished Service Order and the ship herself would receive the Croix de Guerre honour on September 11th 1950.

For the remainder of 1942 and into the middle of 1944 the Felix Roussel trooped between Suez - Bombay - Durban - Australia. From the summer of 1944 into 1945 the ship ran between the Clyde, Liverpool and Port Said, Gibraltar & Algiers, with occasional trips to Freetown & Bombay. She arrived back from a Suez run in November 1945 and then loaded up with what was to be her final cargo of troops and Prisoners of War, sailing from Liverpool, bound for Durban, on Christmas Eve 1945, the voyage my father joined. Thereafter she was returned to her owners in April 1946, who ran her as a liner in the Far East until 1955 when she was sold for $3.5 million to the Arosa Line of Panama and renamed the Arosa Sun. She was refitted in Trieste for Atlantic service and ran a liner service across the North Atlantic until 1958 when she was seized at Bremen due to the Arosa Line's outstanding debts. Bankruptcy followed and the ship was auctioned off in 1960 to Koninglijke Nederlandsche Hoogoven & Stalfabrieken, to become a floating hostel for steel workers at Ymuiden, Holland. In 1974 she arrived at Bilbao to be broken up for scrap.

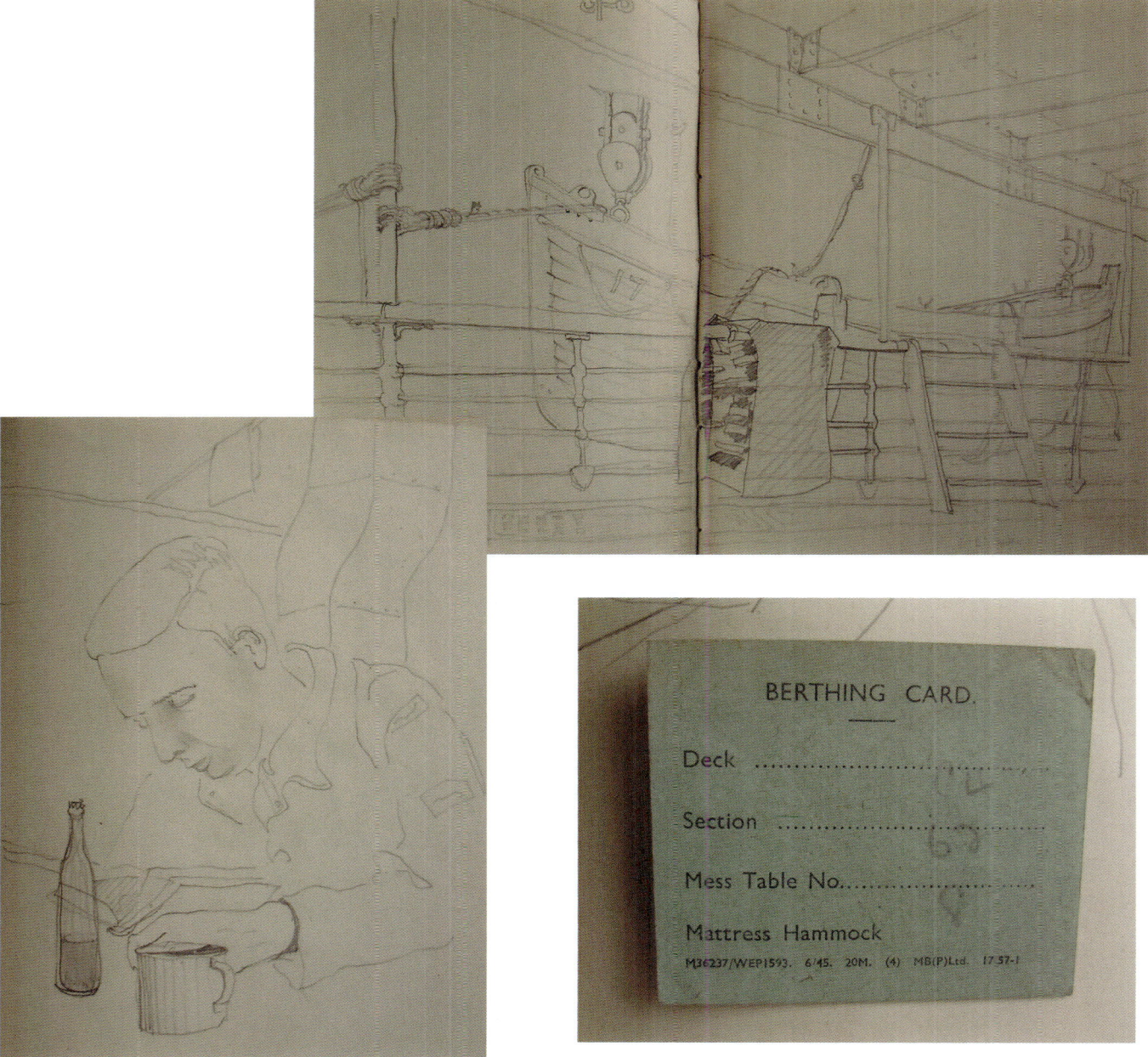

Life on board the troopship

Postcard of the Felix Roussel [Author's collection]

Ian wrote two letters to Pat whilst on the troopship which he joined probably on 23rd December, as she sailed on 24th. The first, which was started on 27th December 1945 a few days after boarding the ship, was 30 sides of small note paper, and probably posted when the ship called in at Taranto to discharge the Italian prisoners of war.
The second, of 17 sides, posted sometime in January after they had arrived at Kasfareet.

The ship was crammed with troops bound for postings in the Middle East and Far East and also a large contingent of civilian (probably civil servants) men, women and children returning to their former homes in the Empire, and Italian PoWs being returned home. Given her heroic role in the evacuation of Singapore, ironically, she may even have been carrying some of those same civilian refugees back there again. However, there was a segregation system as the troops were not meant to mix with the 'posh' civilian passengers. The troops had to do duty standing guard at the connecting door between the two parts of the ship to keep the troops out of civilian areas. My father breaks off from a letter to go on this guard duty from 5.30 to 7.30 one evening:

> "There are a perfectly ghastly set of female passengers aboard who parade up and down the deck in the mornings, get themselves booked for the day and then settle down to a day of line-shooting and goo-gooing to the 1st class passengers who are invariably pickled. There are two French pilots, one with died [sic] blonde hair over his collar, German jackboots on, short shorts, American decorations, PAF[13] wings, a gigantic pair of sunglasses. The other a most unimpressive sort of bloke."

---

[13]Polish Air Force

Beneath the Radar

Another RAF man[14] travelling on a troopship earlier in the war described the cramped conditions in the messdecks:

> "This is where we ate and slept. I think it was twelve men to a table and meals were collected in bulk from a central kitchen by whoever from the table was rostered for the task. At night we collected a hammock from a store at the end of the mess hall and slung the hammock from hooks located above our table. In the morning we had to roll up the hammock which had your number and return it to the store. Once all the hammocks had been slung there was not much room between them and people who snored or emitted other noises were not very popular."

Conscious that life on the home front was still pretty grim, Ian was apparently feeling a bit guilty that the ship had given them a reasonable Christmas, at which point the ship was, ironically, almost exactly opposite his old home in Aberystwyth, Wales. They were given lots of beer to cheer everyone up and wash down a Christmas menu of turkey, stuffing, roast potatoes, greens, butter, two pieces of Christmas pudding about two inches square each. However, this was winter in the Irish Sea, so a lot of the appetites were affected by its notoriously rough weather, and a scare with a near-miss from a floating mine. The pitching and rolling of the ship was obviously making many of the passengers seasick but they were expected nevertheless to fall into a shipboard military routine of guard duties and fatigues.

---

[14] My Service Years. Jock Cassells, The RAM.
https://www.radschool.org.au/magazines/Vol61/Page7.htm

He found everyone else's sickness both amusing and disgusting and it must have been hard to avoid the smell of it all in such crowded mess decks. He only felt really nauseous:

> "… when I get up in the morning and the for the rest of the day I just had headaches, when she really started to wallow I had got quite used to things and quite enjoying seeing horizon listing to an angle of 45 and plates crashing, hammocks swinging, falling down stairs, odd colours of peoples faces. "

The occasional duties onboard were insufficient to keep the troops from deep boredom and, although my father would have done a lot of reading, that soon had him reporting being "cheesed off already". "It is not all easy going, as we have to get up at an ungodly hour". At breakfast:

> "half the people eating, the other lazy half getting out of hammocks, feet walking about amongst ones porridge and bread, food, dangling ropes, faces, hammocks falling, Italians cleaning the floor. Quite amusing in an annoying sort of way!"

The early start made for a "hellish long day". Chess and cards were played endlessly, then "a bit of reading, a walk around the decks when the rain packs up" The mix of mealtime and hammocks was repeated in the evening:

> "the putting up of hammocks is just one quick sprint for the ceiling. Up go the hammocks straight after tea – people all amongst [the] teacups. butter, bread, people walking all over the tables [and] clothes".

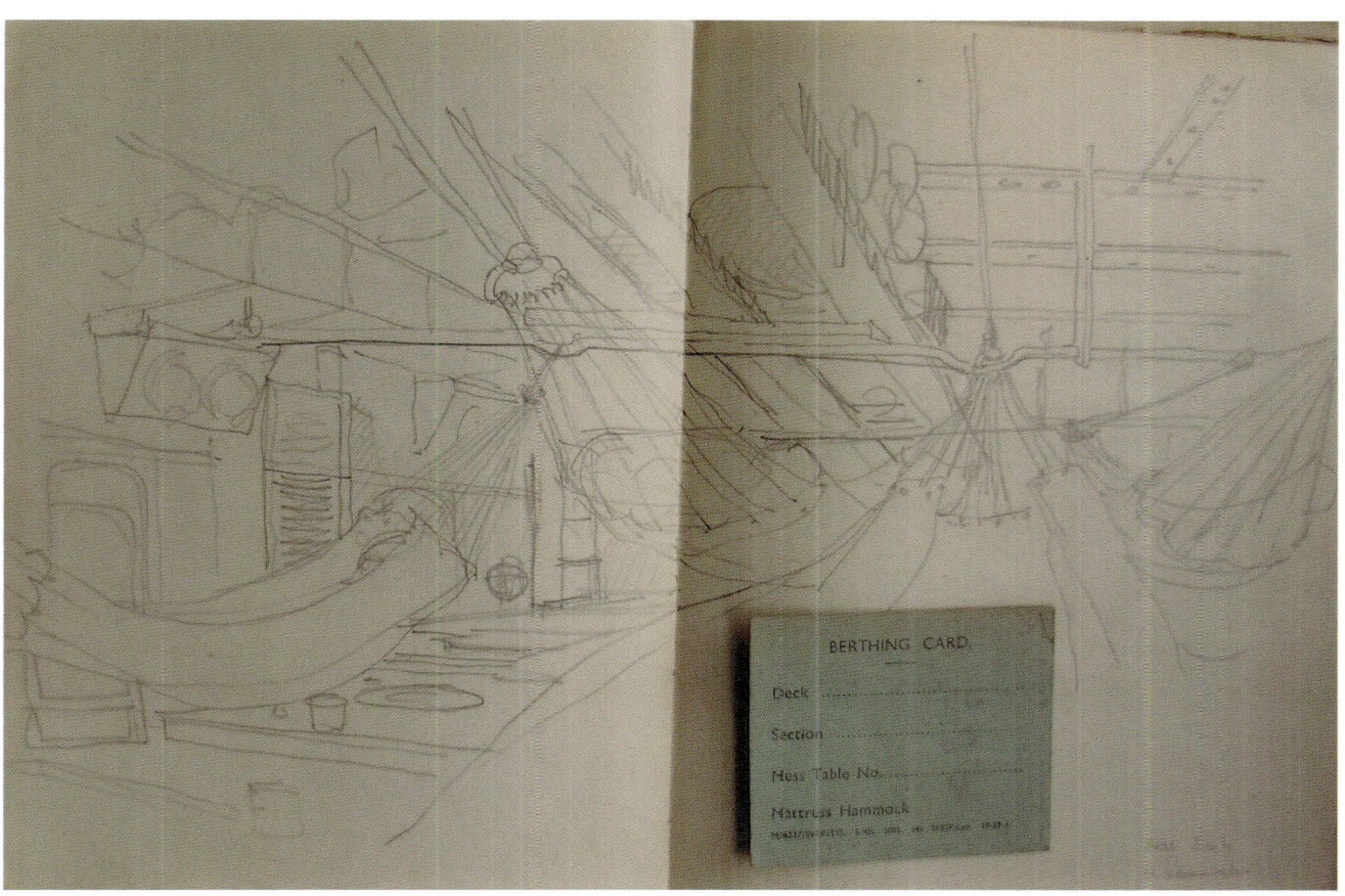

Although he was allocated a hammock space, the air just below the deckhead[15] became hot, stuffy and smelly from the vents and he sometimes chose to sleep on the deck of the mess, saying that was probably safer anyway, since "hammocks can always tip up!"

The food, however, was one of the high points, with astonishing amounts of butter, sugar and other foods served up at every meal but which were of course still rationed at home:

> "We get tons of butter with every meal including dinner. Fags, milk, chocolate are all ridiculously cheap. It makes me mad to think people skimp themselves at home when we have to almost give it away to the Italians so as not to waste it. They wash up for us for 20 fags a day[16] and tailor ones clothes for a few cigarettes and those khaki drill [shorts] need some tailoring too. ... ... The Italians had a colossal black market going where the purchasing power lies in the amount of cigarettes you have got. As cigs are 1/3d[17] per 50 you can get quite a lot done. I had all my laundry done for 25 cigs. Of course they will get about 15/-[18] for 20 in Italy, but still the poor swine live like sardines in pigsties ... ... a breakfast of liver and butter thrown down the gullet to get on deck and see the sights".

---

[15] Deckhead is the nautical term for what a land-person would call the ceiling.
[16] The troops were in 'messes', in the maritime tradition: a group of men sharing a long table and sleeping on, above, around and below it. Each man took turns to be on mess duty each day, collecting food, clearing up and so on. It would be for this group of men in one mess that the Italian PoWs were cleaning up.

[17] 1 shilling and 3 pennies, about 7pence in modern sterling currency.

[18] 15 shillings, 75 pence in modern sterling currency.

Beneath the Radar

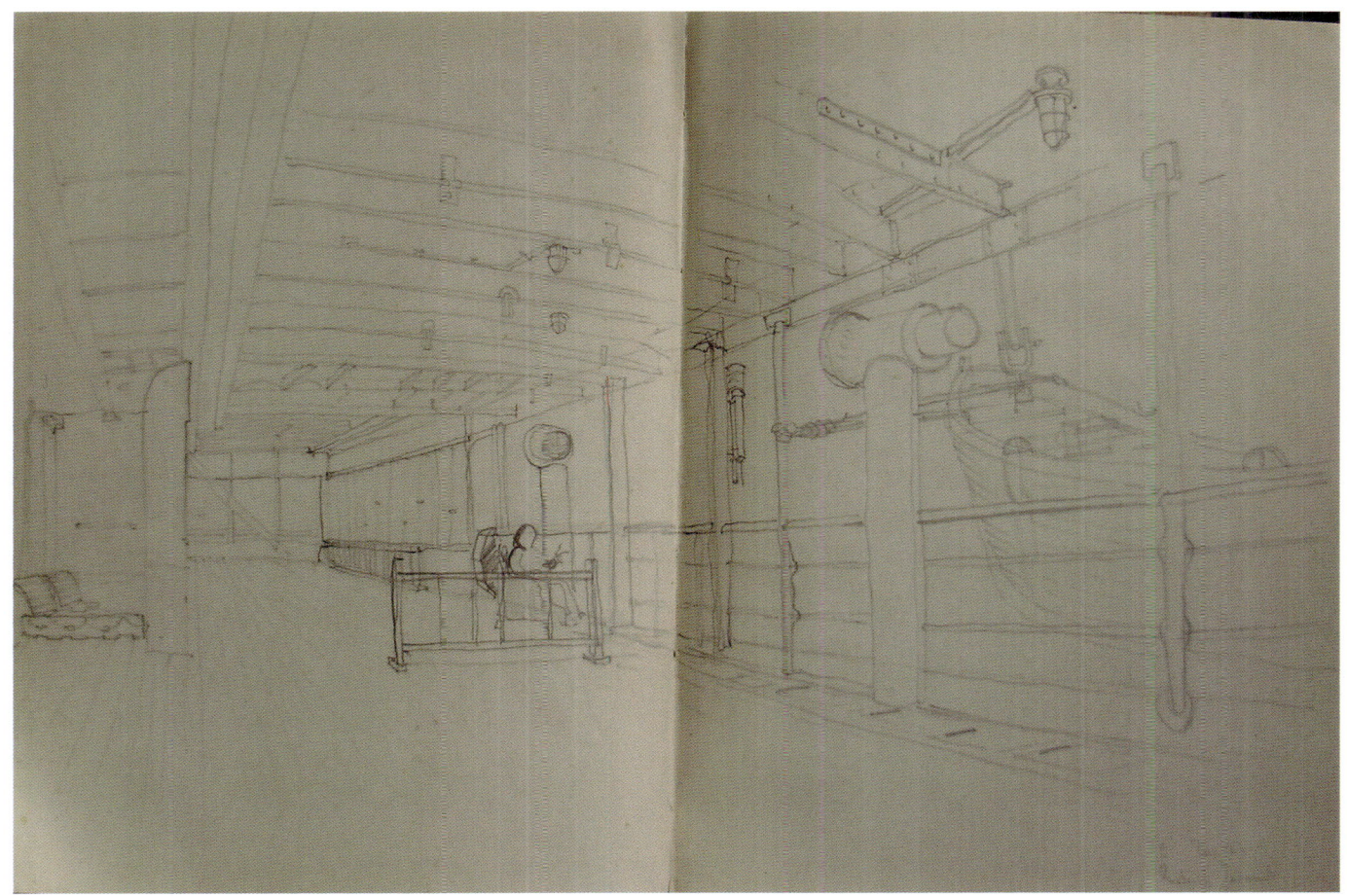

As the troops got further from home, so the Italian PoWs were getting nearer to **their** homes and the British troops often went to their messdecks to listen to their singing, accompanied by violins, guitars and accordions, to such an extent that the messdecks would be packed with men smoking and the smell sometimes drove Ian back up on deck for fresh air. The improvised entertainments put on by the troops for their own amusement proved of a far better quality than the official concerts put on by the ship, which he described as 'grim'. There was a film nearly every night, darts matches, whist drives and so on were organised by the authorities, but the Italians were considered to be the best entertainment on board.

Although the unit was assembled and trained together before leaving the UK, the enforced confinement at close quarters in the ship allowed them to get to know each other much better, and Ian reported that he had come to the decision that there were only 4 others that he liked in the unit. By the time they were all demobbed it becomes apparent that they were all irritating each other quite a lot but, at this early stage, relationships were friendly enough. Many chess games were evidently passing the time on the voyage, but losing one would put Ian in a bad mood – a competitive streak not apparent in Ian's later life. His drawing has clearly come to the attention of the authorities as he has:

> "just been rated for the ship's newspaper and I've got to do a strip for the children every day and it's a bit of a bind because I've got a lot of other things to do like writing a decent letter home [to his parents], which I haven't started yet. I am sure it won't amuse the kids at all."

Left: On deck at sea.
Below: Ian, 3rd from left, with his unit on the troopship

All they heard of the New Year celebrations was:

> "the midnight broadcast from London, Trafalgar Square, with millions of hysterical men and women screaming into the mike. But as a matter of fact I was on guard at midnight guarding the 1st class companionway to stop people getting into or out of the 1st class decks. So I had a pretty painful hour and a half watching and listening to the antics of the drunken civilians and nauseating officers. Of course absolutely nothing at all was done for the ranks, who had two bottles of beer and a rather second rate singsong, compared with the dancing and drinking which was lashed out to the 1st class. In fact it made me thoroughly sick, but anyway we raided the kitchens and had some coffee and biscuits. ... ... The more I think of festivals the more I want to spend them away from London and people."[19]

There is a slightly out of focus photo of my father and what I assume is his immediate unit, all with their lifejackets in hand, taken on deck on New Year's Day. Since I have found other, very similar, small group photos on the internet, taken on the ship on the same day, it looks as though each unit group was set up in turn for these. They anchored off various places en route and Ian took advantage to do sketches from the ship of bits of Italian coastline.

---

[19] Actually, this is more or less what he tried to do very often. The Christmas and new year period was always very quiet in our family and often spent away from the UK.

Taranto harbour

"The Italian Black market was operating as soon as we dropped anchor in Taranto, for a swarm of small row boats (they row standing up here) was soon surrounding the ship. You could sell 50 cigarettes for 10/- in English. Anyway stuff was being hoisted in and out of the windows and portholes all the afternoon - wine, soap, sugar, 10/- notes on the end of pieces of string, the people on the top decks had a hose going by the end of the day to keep them off the ship as some of the crew were selling our cigarettes from the stores in 1,000 packets at £5 a time. Someone got a bright idea of selling empty tins wrapped in cellophane and full of wet paper, but they were smarter and only sent up a shilling.

"We got rid of all the Italian prisoners in a few hours - 2,000 of them - and were expecting the ship to be comparatively empty but by the morning of the next day thousands of S. Africans (all sorts) were pouring on board in all stages of drunkenness and I should think with the beards they had they had been travelling for days.

"There doesn't seem to be any more room in the ship even now, in fact our mess deck seems to be even more crowded than ever. There was a hell of a row at lunch over the amount of food lashed out: a piece of meat and two potatoes and a slice of apple. Someone flung a few sarcastic remarks at the inspecting officer, and it soon started up..... anyway there was an improvement at breakfast this morning which was the worst yet. The first class civil servants get chicken quite frequently.... ... The food queues are a ridiculous length and we spend more and more of each day [in them].

> Eating and getting into bed are the only nice thing that happen all day. There's nothing to see because it's raining, too much noise and mucking about to read. Everything develops into one long argument and biting off of peoples heads. The sight of people playing cards is becoming more and more frequent each day."

Two days later things clearly picked up on the food front, as he got 2 eggs and a rasher of bacon for breakfast plus a pot of Hartleys strawberry jam which he hoped to make last until disembarkation, although he is fed up because he went to buy food for the other 'bods' in the mess and they didn't pay him back fully.
On their last night aboard there was a show:

> "run by the crew and a few of the blokes. It wasn't bad. You know, the usual sort of thing: accordions, women floating about making themselves even more repulsive than I thought they were, but still the mass seemed to have had the time of their lives. A woman recited a whole act of Twelfth Night, which was funny."

Souvenir brooch which the posh passengers presumably could buy

Ferry at Taranto

The Voyage

The Felix Roussel sailed from Liverpool on Christmas Eve, Monday 24th December 1945. The ship's movement card does not record it but she only made it 8 miles out of harbour before having to turn back due to a burst oil feed pipe in the engine room, until amid "…much broken English and French we sailed again at 02.25 on Tuesday morning." This elderly ship was really struggling by the time of this voyage and the movement card records many repairs on this last voyage before she was handed back to her owners. This was her very last voyage to the Far East as a troopship for the Allies, prior to being returned to her civilian role.

They hit a bad storm off the southern end of Ireland, when the nausea turned to headaches in my father's case. They passed Cape St Vincent during enough daylight for him to see the coast with a great hill with trees and off-white houses, but unfortunately passed the Straits of Gibraltar during the night of 29th December. No letters were to be dropped off when they passed Gibraltar so the letter got fatter and fatter as Ian added to it at intervals for posting on the ship's arrival at Taranto. The letter from the troopship was started on Thursday 27th December, by which time the ship was off the Portuguese coast, which Ian reports as being very much like their views of the Welsh coast a couple of days previously, except that "The sky is deep red behind it and the hills seem to be flaked with white".

Beneath the Radar

They woke up on the morning of 30th December to Gibraltar's lights passing 10 miles off:

> "Spanish mountains stretched behind in a black mass…. ... The sea was blue black, almost black and the sky perfect blue. The rock itself looks like a pile of mottled sand against the grey Spanish mountains behind and just a bit disappointing." On the other side of the ship "is Tangier. We can just see the houses of the town. Behind it rises a colossal mountain 4 or 5 times the size of Gib, golden red in the sun, mistey [sic] round the base and a thin streamer of cloud floating off the top."

This was evidently very picturesque and of course he longed to share more than the word description with Pat. All his letters are full of apologies for his handwriting but also for what he saw as his poor way with words. He probably did more writing during this year of his life than he ever did again.

At last, they started to get better weather, once in the Med, and the winter sun sufficient to cause some sunburn and cheer everyone up. Suddenly the trip seemed idyllic and

> "Lying flat on the deck I would like this journey to go on for ever. Bags of porpoises and big black herring gulls following the ship in a perfectly calm day... .... I am excited about what lies ahead. Everyone is in very high spirits and talk runs high all day".

Beneath the Radar

As they sailed along the Algerian coast there was much to admire:

> "... reached Algiers itself at about 10 o'clock the sun was behind it, but by the time we came round the point we could see the sun shining on the tight mass of white squares dotted with windows the town itself spreads over a large area of hillside fringing the water and the houses themselves spread out from the base upwards to a height of 5 or 600 feet. Towards the end of the town there are large blocks of white flats 6 or 7 stories for which I think Algiers is quite famous? Way back over the hill of Algiers the Atlas Mountains spread higher and higher and behind them I suppose the desert. The actual land itself is quite green but I imagine for most part very sparsely occupied. But the sun looked really good shining on the houses and odd mosques or whatever they are called out in this part of the world. We kept to the coast all the way after that, massive mountains all the way coming straight out of the sea, grey black and brown, a wee bit depressing when you see about 200 miles of it. It is another 500 miles to Bizerte and Cape Bon where we turn north to Malta and Taranto, calling at Taranto on Tuesday night, docking on Wednesday morning. 4 days there then off to Port Said, at least another 4 or 5 days sailing."

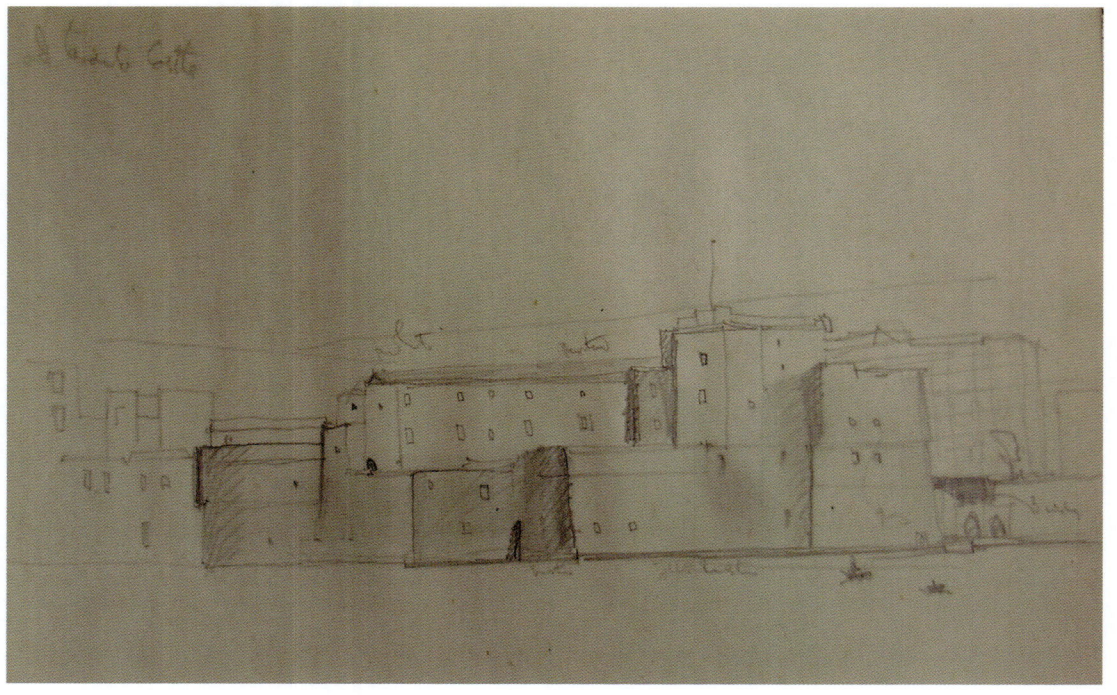

The idyll of the past couple of days abruptly changed to nausea-inducing storms:

> "God, people are going green and grey again – I think I will get in my hammock as it is the only thing that stays perpendicular on this ship!" The next morning was New Year's Eve and the weather had turned into a "marvellous morning, the sun has steamed the decks dry... ...I've got to live where there is sun all the time but I expect I will soon tire of the heat", but still with a rough sea "and this tub is still shaking badly".

Passing Cape Bon they turned north towards Malta, somewhat behind time because the ship could only do about 10 knots.

They did not actually see Bizerte due to being too far offshore, but were impressed by passing a

> "huge hunk of rock with masses of queer shaped pinnacles on it, sheering straight up out of the sea about 1000 feet, black as pitch with the sun behind and the deep blue sea in the foreground."

The much-anticipated stopover at Taranto must have been a grim disappointment as only those due to leave the ship there were allowed ashore.

"It looked like being a really good place to explore. We arrived at the Harbour of Taranto in the morning[20] and the rain started to pour as soon as we had put our noses inside the place. It is contained in a big bay and the docks are reached by a large canal running through the centre of the old quarter. We were anchored in the centre of the bay and had a complete panorama of the whole waterfront and it was well worth seeing. Mussolini had erected a gigantic great Castel plum in the middle of the town, punctuated with large holes to represent openings or something like that. Anyway it was very gross and monstrous. The houses on the front were beautiful to look at as a whole, but I should imagine at close quarter not much cop. They varied from every shade of pink to brown the majority of course being white. The old Castel stands at the entrance of the canal and is very bare with minute windows irregularly placed on the facades. We were a bit too far away to get any details of the town, but when the sun eventually did shine, I wouldn't have missed it for all the tea in china (as the idiotic saying goes). I suppose that was nothing, compared with what there is to see in the rest of Italy."

Most of Taranto harbour itself was full of the sunken Italian fleet marked with small buoys.

---

[20] 2nd January 1946, according to the record card, and they sailed on the 3rd January.

Mess 26 MV Felix Roussell

"The ship passed Crete in the afternoon[21], a large range of mountains on the horizon capped with snow. It was 60 miles away so we could not see much. I had no idea it was so mountainous and I also had no idea how long it takes to get to Cairo from Italy."

Anticipation of the next stage in their journey was largely fed by rumour during the voyage, with their emotions swinging from being keen to see these exotic countries, to despondency about how grim the journeys and work were going to be, fuelled by reasonable assumptions of chaos at the various depots en route and not expecting to be in Palestine before the end of January (writing on 7th January 1946) – and hence the flow of mail to Patricia would be interrupted.

---

[21] Probably around 5th or 6th January as they arrived in Port Said on 7th January, according to the ship record card.

Palestine, Jordan, Egypt and Libya

The first staging post in the Middle East would be El Mayan camp, some 7 miles from Cairo, which was clearly quite an attractive proposition with its evident opportunities for sightseeing trips into the city. However, their first job of work would be to get the crated-up camp to somewhere in Palestine and then erect it in the dead of winter. The journey was expected to begin with:

> "… a 3 or 4 day trip in the wagons across the Sinai desert and then finding the place, building camp, which will take 4 or 5 days of bloody hard work." He had a "nice short raincoat specially adapted to me, dust proof and bug proof according to the pamphlet issued with it.... ... we've got to get our kit up from the hold and draw our arms etc. Guns even have to get cleaned on a ship."

The unit brought together in the UK and shipped together on the Felix Roussel was still apparently incomplete:

> "...we haven't even got a CO yet, or a cook. You can bet it will be a massive carve-up at Helwain[22]... ... but I don't much mind how long we stay there because the Palestine place is grim according to people who know".

---

[22] I think 'Helwain' and 'El Mayan' mentioned in the letters and artwork must be the camp and town more usually spelled Helwan.

Beneath the Radar

El Maya transit camp

Even before they left the ship, El Karak camp was not anticipated happily and Ian was "...not looking forward to arriving in to Egypt and putting that blasted camp up. We've got a very long trip up to Palestine in the wagons too." The first letter after disembarkation from the troopship was sent from Kasfareet, a transit camp near the Suez Canal, on 8th January 1946. First impressions were, as to be expected, of the heat and dust.

The arrival in Port Said coincided with my father having to do 'breakfast duty' so he missed:

> "... all the preliminary excitement of the first sight of land, new sorts of boats, buoys, gulls, different sorts of things floating about in the water. But I did get up [on deck] in time to see the famous sight of Nile fishing smacks going out for the day's haul with their tremendous sails and dark coloured crew with white turbans on. It was a most impressive sight. Always to be seen I suppose and just like the pictures one sees. The men in the boats were looking very miserable compared with the Italians who were grinning all over their faces all the time. They soon vanished into the mist and we rode slowly behind two other large vessels into the harbour. I was expecting a rather black and dirty place for a port, but the first thing we saw was a long white beach with miles of coloured bathing huts and sunshades, a row of trees, two or three rows of palms and then a long line of rather Americanised flats, hotels, expensive looking villas, flat roofs predominating. The whole place, from the distance we were [at], looking rather gold in colour and the pink (pale) Egyptian brick predominates the whole. Most of the stucco used around here is a sort of yellow ochre colour.

Beneath the Radar

"Out came the rowing boats crammed tight with bags, suitcases, wallets, cushions and those 'poof things' Roger[23] sent home. Great exchanges went on £6 for cases but nothing at any reasonable price. All the stuff very trashy. We spent our cash on wolfing down Turkish delight, dates, oranges, but our financial state soon put a stop to this. Most of us are down to our last 25 piastres which is about 4/-[24] or so. After watching the masses of boats around the ship all day, people coming and going, the perfectly speckles whiteness of the ferries (dozens of them), we disembarked in an LST[25] which brought back distant memories of cold days of happiness on the Dartmouth ferry. We passed the better part of Port Said with its flashing neon signs and lights and arrived at the station to experience the first real 'bind' of the east, [people][26] pestering you to buy peanuts, rubber bands, oranges, eggs, watches, spices, books. 'American literature' as it is politely called[27].

---

[23] Roger Rawlinson, my mother's brother. He was a sergeant in the infantry in North Africa and spent some time in Egypt, where he met his future wife, Vivienne, then an ATS cipher clerk. Presumably 'poof things' or pouffes (stuffed leather footrests) were an exotic novelty in those days.

[24] 4/- = Four shillings sterling = 20p. The Egyptian currency was then 100 piastres to the Egyptian pound.

[25] LST = Landing Ship Tank, the military forerunner of today's roll-on roll-off ferry. See http://en.wikipedia.org/wiki/Landing_Ship,_Tank We cannot know which one of these craft was in use then but there is a good chance it was HMS LST 3041 http://en.wikipedia.org/wiki/LST_3041

[26] I have done some editing of my father's writing as some of the terms he used would not be acceptable to today's readers. He never, I think, had a racist thought in his life, but I guess his language then would have reflected the norms of those times.
[27] Perhaps we can assume this was euphemism for pornography?

"Then into the station which was a typical ramshackle affair for such a [significant?] place as Port Said. The smell... ... at first it knocks you back in its intensity, it's a cross between two or three thousand people chewing garlic and a chicken hutch a week old. I was just beginning to wonder what they wear under those white night shirts down to their ankles, when a kid whipped his off and ran screaming into a shallow bit of water.

"The CO, meanwhile, nearly got lynched for offering a bloke half a piaster to carry his bags. What with all the kit and smells, excitement of the day etc., we were all feeling pretty tired when we piled into the grim looking carriage of metal, with wooden seats, very high off the ground with no glass in the windows. The station by now was just a mass of screaming kids, men, animals, dust, clanging of bells, and the monotonous chanting of various pedlars and beggars. On our other side, just for interest, were a few hundred tommies packed into cattle trucks.

"At last the bloody train started and we passed through various evil-smelling halts along the Canal. Massive ships just one mass of lights steaming slowly through the night. After about two hours we reached a place called Ishmalia, change here, more sweating with kit, more Egyptians. An hour to wait, a meal in a NAAFI. Streets dark and then you would come across a whole street of cafes and lighted stalls just swarming with smelly people chanting, eating etc.

"We beat a hurried retreat when a horrible looking individual came up and asked if we wanted to see his sister. He got really fierce when we said we weren't interested. But still I enjoyed every minute as it was our first real sight of the actual living conditions out here. Although it was about 11 at night we haven't seen a single woman (Egyptian I mean) yet. Except one who was carrying a colossal load of bags, bedding, kids etc, with the husband, quite small, walking along in front carrying a small bell. God knows what for, but it was quite amusing to see."

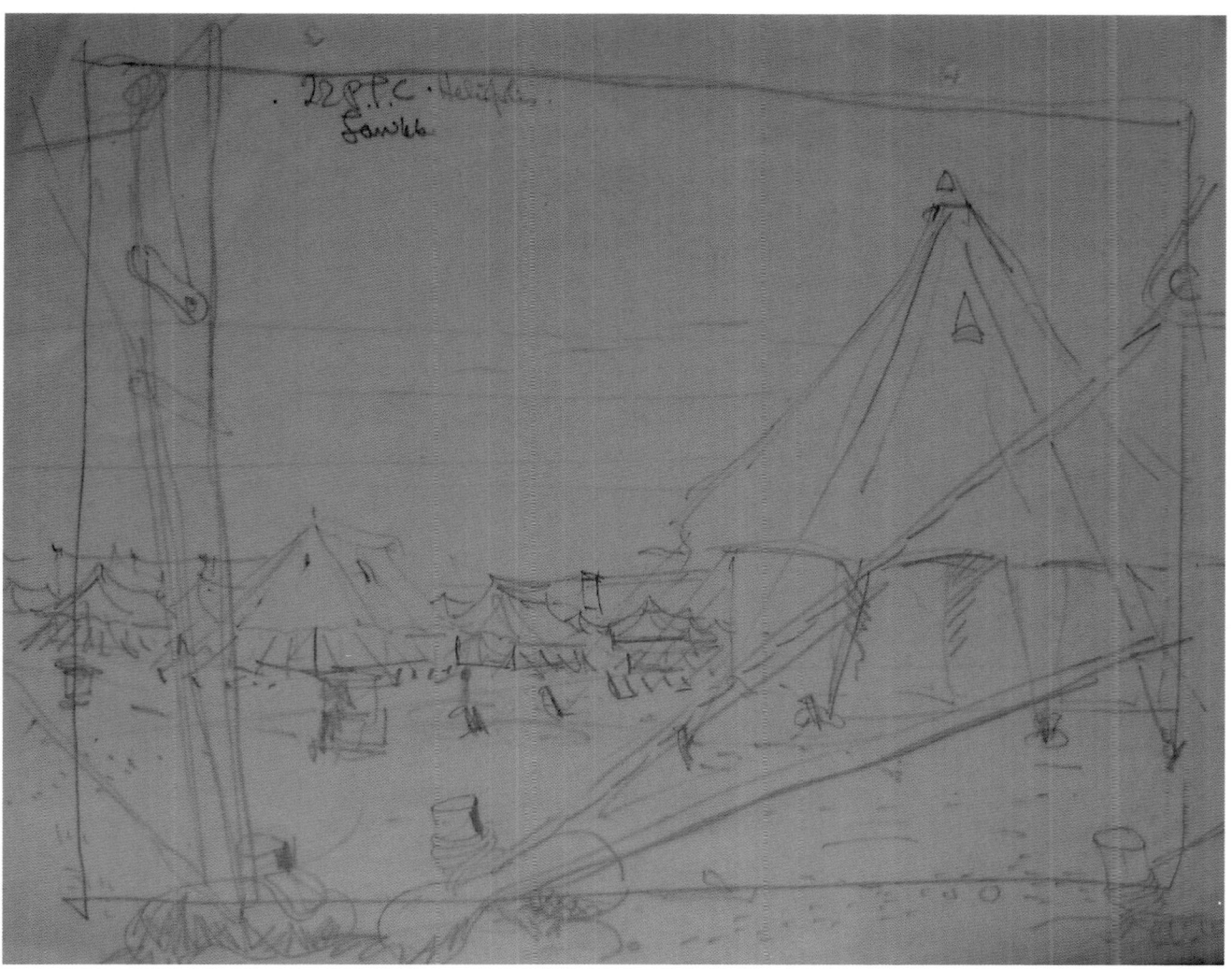

Life in camp

They arrived at their first transit camp, Kasfareet in the small hours of 8th January 1946:

> "... we got to our tents about 3.30 after a great deal of mucking about. In the morning we woke to see desert, tents, wire and mountains in the distance. This place is as flat as it could be, with water and palms about a mile off, masses of camp with miles of tents, miles to walk everywhere. My bed is quite comfortable. Quite a good canteen with cream cakes, pukka icing, which I have been eating all day... ... I couldn't resist the temptation although I haven't got used to the [Egyptian] flavour in the food yet. I know I should be buying gifts but I don't think we shall come across anything like shoes, stockings etc till we get to a place like Cairo or Palestine. We go, I think, to Helwain after this but at the moment there is a 'gear' muck up as they don't know what we are."

Evidently the system took some time to catch up with them as the mail didn't arrive for a while and then Ian got 20 letters all at once, which are apparently by this point all being sent to them by air. The advantage is that they get to enjoy the tourist experience in Cairo. It was:

Pete in his pit, El Maya

"... a real eyeopener. I was quite shaken by the state of affairs regarding goods, prices, shops, food etc in the big city. The town itself is as badly put together as London. There is the central part of shopping centres, main streets, cinemas, government buildings surrounded by the [native] quarters which occupy ¾ of the area – out of bounds to us of course. The main street, Suleiman Pasha, has a strong American tang about it. Shop fronts small but neat, bags of chrome. Some very large shops stocked with international goods etc. I hadn't the time to discover the pukka prices for shoes and clothes but men's shoes are all about £2. What I saw of women's shoes weren't really good, I did see some for about £4. The camera situation is good and the prices are falling so I hope that when I get back from my 6 months tour of Palestine they will be even cheaper. Films are about 5/-.

... People out here seem to make a living selling watches and cameras, making leather bags and selling them. The fashionable zip two handled bags are in great demand out here – you can get a really big one for £6-8 and smaller for £2. The clothes are quite good, mostly Americanised, especially the men's. The women's shops seem to tend to the French styles as there is a large amount of French spoken here and I imagine the French population out here is nearly as big as the British. French books everywhere. The book situation is good and the stuff out here would make your eyes drop out... ... all the magazines, Life etc, unobtainable in Britain at £2 out here."

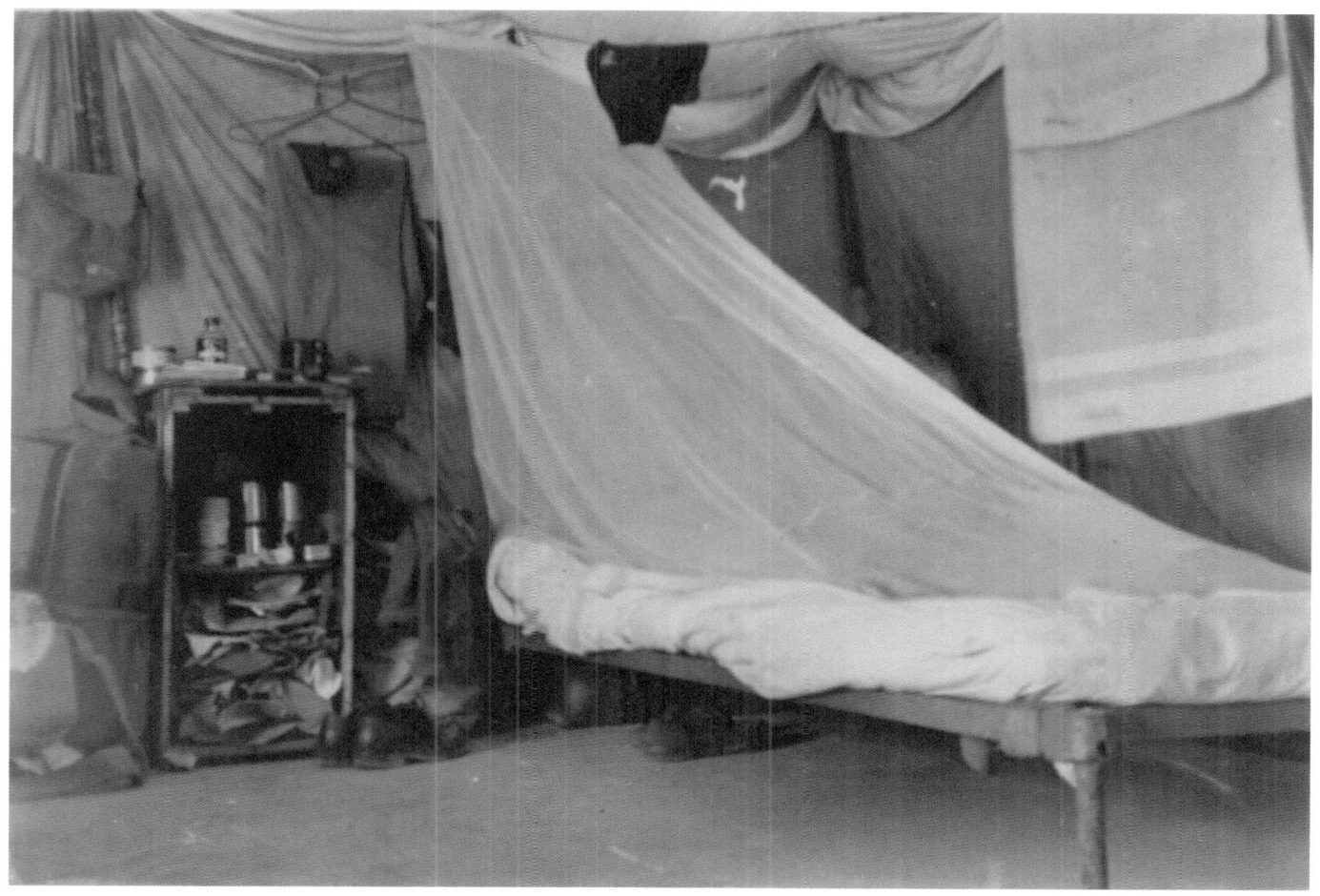

Bed space in tent, with mosquito net. [Ian Baker]

"Our arrival here clashed with the visit of King Saud of Arabia who is visiting[28] [King] Farouk, so we have seen Cairo at its best – masses of lights at night, most of the shops have neon and the streets are a mass of neon lights almost comparable with Oxford Street. The traffic is grim with few traffic lights only hooters are used to scream all over the place. I have nearly been killed twice looking left instead of right crossing the road the traffic drives the other way of course which takes some getting used to. Very few buses in fact practically none at all."

He discussed with my mother a plan to save hard while the unit was on the road and spend all the money on desirable items unobtainable back home before he returned to the UK. He was able to send packages of dates back to his family, via the NAAFI, and the bookshops were far better stocked with high quality art books and prints than he had been able to find at home. Horse-drawn vehicles could be hired for touring the city, at 85 piastres for a day. However, the Padre apparently organised tourist trips for the troops, to the Pyramids, tombs, on the Nile, Old Cairo etc, which were reckoned a good deal.

---

[28] Saud was visiting Egypt's King Farouk to discuss the "Palestinian question" 10-16 January 1946 http://www.ibnsaud.info/main/3681.htm and a news reel at http://www.britishpathe.com/record.php?id=55590

Ian on the left in both pictures, at Gizeh

It is possible that these trips were being organised to try to improve morale amongst RAF personnel as this was the period when there were actual strikes[29], formally mutinies, amongst RAF men in India, Ceylon and Singapore, with thousands refusing to parade and take orders. This arose largely due to a mixture of slow demobilisation, terrible living conditions for the other ranks in some RAF stations India in particular, and an over-bureaucratic attitude by the regular career officers. Many 'emergency only' RAF ranks, knowing the war itself was over, saw no point in the formalities and hated being in hot, largely insanitary conditions with terrible food. Earlier in the war there had been what was known as the "Cairo Forces Parliament", a sub-mutinous discussion group which was allowed to continue by the authorities, and in which many overtly communist and socialist servicemen took part.

So, the North African command must have been nervous of such problems spreading across the RAF bases there and probably did what they could to make life a bit easier for the thousands of RAF men in transit.

---

[29] Mutiny in the RAF: the air force strikes of 1946. David Duncan. Published in the Socialist History Society Occasional Papers Series: No 8, 1998. https://libcom.org/book/export/html/26188 See also this documentary about the mutiny: https://youtu.be/-1SkyxdlSR0

Indeed, the next letter, with the pages numbered in Arabic numbers, is a report of just such a trip: "I went to the Pyramids expecting to be a bit disappointed and discover it was all a bit of a white elephant, but it was as good as you imagine it is in the flics and a lot more besides. To start with, I was expecting it to be lying on a large flat expanse of desert with the Nile or something running beside it. But instead it was standing on a hill, quite a climb in the car

anyway, with a hotel a few hundred yards away, cafe and a car park right at the base of the large pyramid.

"Of course everything is commercialised to a tee and the [Egyptians] spent the whole time trying to get tips off you for this and that. We had a pukka guide to show us round and the party was organised from the camp otherwise you get rooked left and right. To start with we got all the 'gen', you know all the stuff in the guide books etc etc about it being 13 acres square, built in 30 years by so many thousands. Of course there is about 40 foot off the top and it is all irregular, the stones having been taken for the building of various mosques in Cairo. So it is not smooth, in fact it goes up in steps of about 10 feet. It really is immense and the stones are colossal.

"Everything, as everything is in Egypt, is shabby and untidy great hunks of stones, wire, boxes, filth all over the place, actually reminded me of a badly blitzed slag heap. Anyway the walk up to the King's Tomb is tortuous and back breaking, through passages up a very rickety stairway which was very rotten and about 50 feet high and 4 feet wide. The King's Chamber is an empty room with a rather decrepit looking stone box, which once contained his remains. You don't get into the other Pyramids at all. They are shallow of course and further to walk too.

"We next saw the terrific stone ramp that led at one time down to the Nile, quite impressive and one could quite easily imagine the masses of slaves pulling and heaving the stones up the ramp. We saw various other small temples, very little left but walls. The guide [was] taking great delight in showing us some rather nauseating hieroglyphics as we went into various very dirty underground caverns which were once great tombs of queens, prime ministers, but the candles kept going out so we didn't see much and the day was becoming pretty hot and sticky and I was becoming cheesed off because I wanted to see the Sphinx. I had one or two snapshots of myself taken on the stones with sphinx, pyramids etc in background. We reached the Great Sphinx from the back end which rather spoils the whole effect as his face was hidden in a dark shadow. He or she faces east and it was 2 o'clock so I was quite happy looking at shadows and wondering what it looked like when it was whole. But I was beginning to get that feeling of weariness[30] that one gets in museums of seeing too much and walking too far.

"I had seen plenty and enjoyed every minute of it really but as always you can never expect everything to be exactly as you would like it to be. Anyway we had a very good tea and cream cakes, tips paid for by the RAF, transport provided too, so it was quite a success. Some didn't think so but I did!"

The tour must have been something of a highlight, as most of the time the unit seems to have been lying about in their tents:

---

[30] Known in the Baker family as 'museumitis', when your legs are weary and your brain cannot absorb any more.

"...doing quite a bit of drawing, reading not to mention film shows, eating etc. I was out drawing a mosque this afternoon when of course I was surrounded by the usual onlookers you get anywhere. I had a hell of a time with a native who wanted to show me his monkey (very evil smelling) play with his pet snake (also very evil and slimey!). He roared with laughter when I said I would fetch a policeman - most disconcerting. I tried my hardest to get rid of him, swearing, not taking any notice, in the end he was becoming such a bind I got up and started to move and he just disappeared."

Ian also visited a mosque, although the original plan had been to visit the Cairo Museum but he and his friends became lost and two local boy scouts offered to taken them to the King's Palace. When that proved to be closed the scouts took them to the mosque as a 'good deed'. Ian found the massive mosque very impressive, with "hardly anything not covered with gold mosaic and tons of ivory work, mother of pearl covering the walls, which towered up to a 200 foot dome with nothing on the face to spoil the effect of the size and enormity of the place." This is followed by a detailed description of this 75-year old mosque, and even a sketch plan. Ian felt the atmosphere was similar to the Roman Catholic Cathedral in London. They also visited a more dilapidated mosque with massive gold doors, that was about 200 years old.

These visits to Cairo were inhibited by lack of funds and it is apparent that the 'system' had not really caught up with them as Ian's unit were kept in the transit camp for quite a while, with no 'gen' (information) about their move to Palestine.

Beneath the Radar

Palestine

For all the concern about what Palestine might be like, Ian's group were not there very long and there is only one letter from this period. It is unclear when they went to Palestine and the only letter from there was sent from Amman sometime before 14th March 1946, but they were there during a very important period of change for the country. On the 22nd March the ruler of Transjordan, Emir Abdullah I, negotiated a new treaty with the British, under which the Emirate of Transjordan (previously part of the British Mandate of Palestine) gained full independence and became the Hashemite Kingdom of Transjordan. This was the time when the Stern Gang and others from the Jewish campaign for a Jewish state were attacking the British in Palestine and later in the summer the bombing of the King David Hotel took place. None of this background appears in the letter.

The other piece of documentation that survives is a receipt for Ian's contribution to making good some destruction in their barrack hut in Amman. From the date it would seem that there was some sort of junketing before they left Palestine for Libya, as a stove flue pipe and some sheeting plus labour costs had to be paid for.

```
                    Received from 1801109 LAC BAKER,
LP.2093 (Two Pounds Palestinian & 93 mils) in respect
of barrack damages in Building No.29, made up as follows:-

        Flue Pipe          -      988 mils.
        Sheeting.          -       22   "
                                 1000 mils.
        33 1/3% increase.         333   "
                                 1333 mils.
        Labour.            -      665   "
                                 1998 mils.
        5% Overhead charge.        95   "
                   Total         2093 mils.


                                       [signature]
                                      Barrack Warden.
                                    RAF Station, Amman.
19th March, 1946.
```

Ian's letter reported that he had travelled, presumably from Amman, to Jerusalem and El Karrok (Al Karak) but that there had been very little mail, possibly because the unit was moving around so much and the mail had got stuck somewhere.

Tripoli harbour in 1946 with Landing Craft (Tank) LCT in the foreground and the hulk of an old sailing ship which had been there since before at least 1943. [Ian Baker]

Palestine and Jordan Top left: Garden at Gesthemane. Top right: Allenby Bridge.
Centre left: Jordan valley. Centre right: King David Hotel.
Bottom row: unknown. [Ian Baker]

Libya

Ian's next letter home, dated 28th March 1946, was from El Maya, 22PTC[31], another vast tented camp on the outskirts of Cairo. It seems that his little mobile unit had attempted to depart for Palestine but that various mess ups with trains had got them as far as the Suez Canal, supposedly awaiting a ship, in the cold with no food or blankets. Then they were to fly but he found his kit would be too heavy for 'the kite' and therefore posted a lot of his books, Architectural Journals etc home.

Colossus class aircraft carrier, with Fairey Firefly aircraft on deck, in Tripoli harbour.
[Ian Baker]

---

[31] 22 Personnel Transit Centre (PT) was at Al Maza, north east of Cairo. Today Almaza Air Force Base Airport is a regional airport for both civil and military use. It was established as a civilian aerodrome, but was partly taken over by the British military, designated RAF Heliopolis and later RAF Almaza.
https://en.wikipedia.org/wiki/Almaza_Air_Base

Meanwhile he had the tedium of night guard on the Motor Transport Pool, "foot slogging in the sand", not well received after all the failed travelling. Ian consoled himself with tangerines, still sufficiently exotic and rare that he was able to send boxes of them to family in the UK. He also had his first-ever drink of Coca Cola which he describes as a "sort of American equivalent of Tizer"!

Confusingly the next letter from Ian to Patricia was also dated 28th March 1946, as with the letter from El Maya when his unit had failed in their attempt to travel. This letter is from Castel Benito, in the Tripolitania part of Libya and he immediately felt he would like the place, perhaps because of its Italian style and its being much cleaner than Egypt had been. After the previous false start the unit's journey from Cairo to Libya was much smoother, having started with a "very special breakfast at Cairo West Airfield", then embarking on a Lancaster, in which there were no seats, even for officers. Everyone was jammed in and Ian found himself in the middle gun turret, which gave excellent views as the flight progressed. Having left Cairo, there was a lot of uninteresting desert, hills and camel tracks and the gun turret perspex dome soon made the heat unbearable so he had to move down to the main fuselage with the others until they landed in Benghazi. There they were all allowed off for a "super-duper meal in the airfield restaurant" while the plane was re-fuelled. It was then Ian's assignment to sit in the rear gun turret, from which there was a disconcerting view of the ground shooting away as the plane took off, "with only a quarter of an inch of perspex between you and the sea thousands of feet below." The sea was such a clear blue that he could easily see the seabed when they were near the coast.

Aircraft at Castel Benito airstrip. [Ian Baker]

GEE

Ian and his group had been sent to help establish a new kind of radio-based navigation system, GEE. GEE was the first 'hyperbolic navigation system', and entered service with RAF Bomber Command in 1942. It measured the time delay between two radio signals, giving a numerical reading to place the receiver on or between the numbered lines on a special chart. Two such readings from different originating radio stations (Master and 2 or 3 Slaves) would produce a fix, with accuracy on the order of a few hundred metres at ranges up to about 350 miles (560 km). The basic principles were the same as those used by its close successors, Decca and LORAN, and now by the satellite-based positioning systems, such as GPS.

The work which Ian's group was to do was to aid in setting up the Tripoli GEE chain, whose headquarters were at Helwan. Before they arrived, units AMES 141-144 had been dispatched to Castel Benito in 27 10-ton trucks, a journey lasting from 7-25 November 1945. His unit, AMES 141 at Castel Benito, was based at the site of the Master station for this group of stations, with the Slave stations at Giado, Tagiura and Mizsa.

If operating Chain Home Low radar to detect incoming enemy air squadrons was at times demanding, operating a GEE station must have been very, very boring. The work involved watching an oscilloscope with a series of blips representing the signals of the master and slaves in order to maintain a very precise time interval between them, as and when there was any 'circuit drift'.

The best explanation of how this all worked is to be found in 'Radar: a wartime miracle' (Latham & Stobbs).

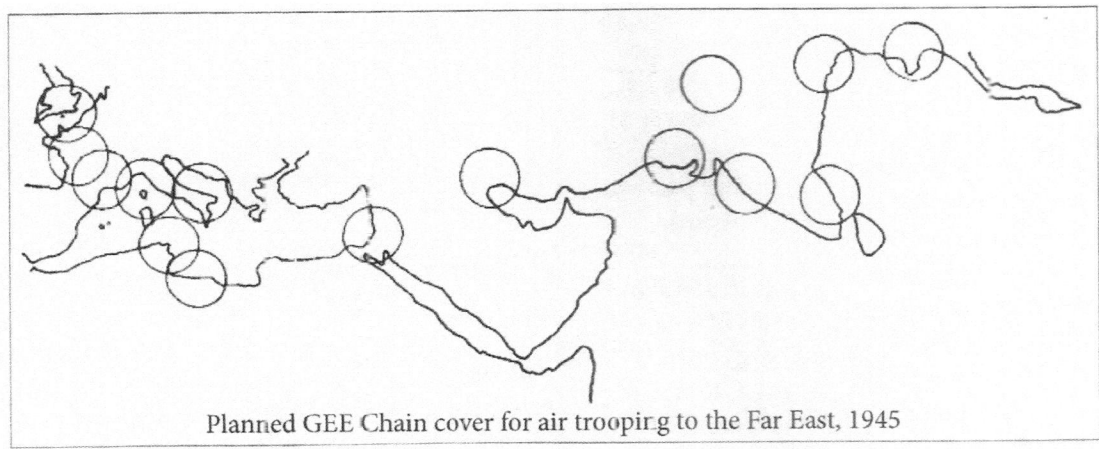
Planned GEE Chain cover for air trooping to the Far East, 1945

The above map is reprinted with permission, from the late W. Blanchard's paper, Overseas GEE Chains 1945/46, in the journal of the Defence Electronics History Society: Transmission Lines Vol 16, no.1, 2011. ISSN 1362-3834

Bu Gheilan Pass, Libya

At each location the group would set up one of the 105-foot sectional towers, build a couple of huts and either operate it for a while or hand it on to operators and then go back for another kit for another location. As the war was already over in Europe at this point, these GEE units were providing a chain of navigational aids to allow Allied aircraft to get from Europe to the Middle and Far East as part of the requirements to bring demobilised service people home after their service was up, and then run the Empire. The Tripoli GEE Chain was to provide the route as far as the Sudan.

Garian

After landing at RAF Castel Benito, Ian's group were accommodated at the airbase for the night before setting off for Garian (Gharyan) the next day:

> "80 kms (60 miles) inland from Tripoli itself, we only saw the outskirts of Tripoli. Dead straight roads for miles then suddenly you start up the hills and through the valleys round the sharpest steepest hairpin bends I have ever seen."

He compared the rocky hills with the similarly bouldery ones in Palestine and was very taken with the views: "… miles and miles of just nothing, it is quite undescribable unless one has seen it oneself."

Bu Gheilan pass, Libya

Ian found Garian to be:

> "... a small village in the mountains, which has more municipal buildings than residents, which typifies these Fascist places as anywhere but England. We are in an abandoned officers (Italian) mess which previous to that was a very nice sanitorium, I should imagine. We, that is myself and my venerable companion 'Bank clerk OAG', have a large room to ourselves about 15'x12' and we [are] at the moment making furniture, plenty of blank walls to draw all over, very pukka washing facilities, everything looking very surgical indeed."

He does not mention it, but Ian must have been aware that Garian's main claim to fame at the time was a massive mural, the Lady of Garian[32], drawn some 3 years previously. The 'Lady' was a reclining nude whose curves had been made to fit the coastline of Libya. This graffiti in one of the barrack blocks might have been why he mentioned that his billet had blank walls suitable for drawing. I have no idea if he did any such drawings and the Lady is not thought to be extant any more.

---

[32] The "Lady of Garian" was drawn by Clifford Saber, a volunteer American ambulance driver with the British 8th Army. Saber created the mural to help boost the morale of his fellow servicemen, finishing on 2 March 1943, while his unit was housed for a few days at the barracks in Gharyan. http://www.ourstory.info/library/4-ww2/Saber/desertTC.html

Work at Garian was watchkeeping on a 24 hour on, 48 hour off cycle, because the radar site was 20 miles from the town. The Chain CO's report[33] for 27th March 1946 mentions that the "Chain is really well settled down operationally now, as the operators have gained the experience required for accurate and breakdown-less operations."

Garian town [Ian Baker]

---

[33] Fl Off Oswald, Operations Record Book for Tripoli Gee Chain, from The National Archives, Kew.

The weather was very cold but off-duty warming up must have been no pain as the town had a small cinema where very cheap drinks (cognac, triple sec, marsala etc) were brought to your seat. This was such a change from "horrible gaseous beer from the NAAFI", that they tried a little of everything on the drinks menu for a total bill of "a couple of bob" (2 shillings or 10p). Ian's billet was very comfortable: "… bed is excellent, sheets and a good laundry, no guards. Horrible paper money and no coins." He was also pleased to find that the commanding officer was the CO from his time at 146[34], whom he regarded as sensible and very nice. Meanwhile, my mother, Patricia, had been demobbed from the WAAF but not found work and was struggling to manage on the 25 shillings a week dole money. In contrast to the First World War, when WRAF women were kept on longer after the armistice in order to let the men get demobbed first, in the Second World War WAAFs were being demobilised even before the armistice.

The work Ian was doing here was the first in quite a long time, what with the travelling and hanging about in the transit camps, but not all that interesting. He did not have to

> "do a great deal. It's just as monotonous as the usual radar and probably a bit more in fact. Anyway it entails keeping awake all night which is a bit of a bind, especially as we do 24 hours straight. The site is right out on the edge of the world, so to speak, with a terrific drop of thousands of feet onto the Tripoli Plain on one side and the Sahara on the other. 3 of us all together and we cook and muck in on everything.

---

[34] The unit at RAF Thame where the group were trained.

Garian Garrison parade ground with aerials in background.

[Ian Baker]

> We eat better up here than down at the Hospital where the food is typical Naafi style meat and same old puddings. I do miss Naafi breaks and tea and we don't have hot water here which means I shall have to [spend] 2 shillings a week to go and have a bath at the hotel opposite, which also does a 3 shilling dinner with wine in the evening which I am trying hard not to make a regular habit."

Other aspects of Garian were less appealing, particularly the colonial attitudes of some of the officers:

> "The Town Major was on parade with his wife this morning, who is almost as corpulent and conceited as he is. All the army people here are 'British Military Authority' and think they are colonial ministers the way they walk about, look with contempt at [our] CO wandering about in a threadbare oily battledress and plimsolls emptying a bucket of refuse into a dustbin.

> The climax of the week is the regular water fight which takes place throughout the building. Great noise and destruction and middle aged men shreiking [sic] like children up and down the stone passages. I suppose it makes a diversion from wasting away in the pit or counting the natives who come in and out of the Administration Building opposite. There are more Administration Buildings in this little place than there are people or houses."

Garian 'Municipio' with Highlanders parading, presumably intended to impress local residents.
[Ian Baker]

Ian's CO was Pilot Officer Eric Amies, whose memoirs[35] of this time give a vivid impression of their work and circumstances. He had been sent out expecting to go to Basra in Iraq but found on arrival in Cairo that plans had changed and in February 1946 he was sent to take over from Flying Officer Pullen at:

> "... one of the four stations of the Tripoli (Libya) GEE chain, AMES 142 at Tagiura, about seven miles east of Tripoli. The master station was at Garian, some 50-70 miles due south of Tripoli with the other 2 sites south and west of that. Garian was a pleasant little town, with the domestic site in an hotel, but the tech site was in very arid and rugged country, as I believe were the other two sites. At Tagiura we lived in an old Italian fort, dating from the time when they took over Libya. Not quite a 'Beau Geste' building but very similar. The tech site was about 2 miles away on a low hill. Unlike the UK chains, which were mainly conceived to provide navigational assistance to aircraft flying over Europe, these were to provide terminal navigation to trooping aircraft approaching airfields along the route. But it rapidly proved impossible to maintain a supply of replacement personnel and the chain closed down in April. After that I went to the nearby airfield at RAF Castel Benito as Radar Officer in charge of the workshop servicing GEE equipment until I was released in October 1946."

---

[35] From privately held archives, kindly shared by Squadron Leader Mike Dean MBE.

The British Military Authority in each conquered zone of the war issued its own money and the money in Tripolitania was issued in lire notes, but apparently no coins as mentioned above. Certainly, a colonial attitude would have been very likely to be prevalent. Indeed, when we think that the British were occupying the buildings and social strata formerly occupied by the previous colonial power, the Italians, it is scarcely surprising that this was the case. The majority of the few people whom Ian saw in Garian appeared to him to be nomadic Arabs, which perhaps explains why there were so few native residents in the town. The buildings which Ian was seeing, including the sanatorium in which they were billeted, probably included some designed by the most prominent Italian architect of the Fascist era: Florestano Di Fausto[36] (1890-1965). Castel Benito was one of a series of 'new villages' which the Italian Fascist colonial authorities (the Tripolitania Colonization Agency) had built for Italian farmers to move into.

---

[36]Florestano di Fausto: https://en.wikipedia.org/wiki/Florestano_Di_Fausto#Libya

Garian [Ian Baker]

Looking towards the Tripoli Plain from Garian

The tiny town of Garian had been built to support an influx of nearly 4,000 Italian families[37] to work for a commercial tobacco enterprise. Presumably most of this colonising effort was quickly ended with the war, although some fundamental damage was done by the introduction of 'modern' agricultural techniques as the European ploughs so destroyed the fragile soil structure that much of the area which had been orchards had become sand dunes, when the World Bank reported[38] on it in 1960. So, it is perhaps no wonder there were so many administration buildings and so few people, as presumably all the Italian colonisers were evacuated at the start of the war and the ruined ecosystem would no longer support even the previous basic lifestyle of the local people.

Having got the Tripoli GEE chain up and running, as mentioned above, on 27th March 1946, it must have been particularly galling for the Chain CO, Fl Off Oswald to have to write in his ORB on 2nd April 1946 that orders had been received to cease operations, start packing up all the technical equipment and await disposal instructions. By 25th April this was proceeding as well as a shortage of packing materials would allow and most was packed, apart from tools and test gear, so it must have been beyond infuriating for Fl Off Oswald to get instructions on 27th April to cease dismantling and report the state of preparedness to resume operating the GEE chain!

---

[37] Libyan new villages: https://dadfeatured.blogspot.com/2019/04/new-villages-in-1940-italian-libya.html

[38] The Economic Development Of Libya. Published For The International Bank for Reconstruction and Development. The Johns Hopkins Press, Baltimore. 1960.

Demonstrating extreme restraint, he reported back that to resume operations would require all the equipment to be transported back from Tripoli, various power supplies to be re-established and new personnel found to replace those departing for their demobilisation. In May the chain was being commanded by Flying Officer Nash and it seems that that was about the end of it, and FO Nash ended the ORB reporting in June that all personnel and equipment had been dispatched from the slave sites to the master site.

Top: lorry on the road somewhere in the Tripolitania plain. [Ian Baker]
Bottom: Ian (centre) with colleagues and dog. [Ian Baker]

Ian's next letter, undated but marked as being the 12th letter, described a day's work in which his group had had to pull things down and dig holes in what was becoming hotter weather, with hot winds roaring in from the Sahara. Presumably this was part of the dismantling reported in the ORB. Although the war was over, relating the specifics of his work still seem to be forbidden and the letter gives no hint as to what is being pulled down. However, he had also had an afternoon to wander about in the valley where he saw "a black and white eagle flying slowly over craggy cliffs", which he was able to follow with his binoculars, before being "scared off by green lizards, large flying ants, and a snake the colour of sand which kept jumping out of the grass in front of me as I stumbled into the steep ravines which the small rivers make in the valley."

Looking down onto Garian town from hill road. [Ian Baker]

The aerial site with radar (GEE trucks) [Ian Baker]

He got quite close to the eagle which brought his walk to the edge of the cliff where he stood on a massive boulder to admire the view of empty countryside spread to the horizon. Sunset came quickly, forcing him to hurry back to the base, stumbling over a nomadic family encampment, which made him feel "very naked and white as I only had on my shorts, shoes and my binoculars, but they only looked and murmured 'Saide' which means something like 'Howdo'". When he got back to the billet it was dinner time and he made lemonade from his own lemons and a spam and potato omelette, which was deemed "quite good". He hoped to get into Tripoli the following day, hoping to buy himself some drawing instruments and ideally for a swim as they do not seem to have access to bathing facilities at this point.

Ian sitting on barracks veranda wall.
[Ian Baker]

Brian "Myself" "Tree-Ape" F/Sgt.

The next letter is dated 26th April. Ian had a number of friends visiting as they passed through Garian on their way to Tripoli, perhaps for their demobilisation. Although busy, it seems that his activities were largely of a leisure nature: socialising with the friends, drawing and painting on the walls, and he seemed to think he would be returning to 'Blighty' in January (1947). My mother Pat was apparently about to go on a course in London, probably the technical drawing course for which her exercise books still exist.

Ian had been cooking himself a meal: an omelette with ham and cheese and chips, finished off with a liqueur called Abtei which he thought to be French, and described as being very potent and evaporating in the mouth a bit like a Benedictine. In the latter comparison he was actually spot on as the liqueur is indeed made by Benedictine monks but it is actually a German herbal liqueur from the Westphalia region, so presumably the local supply had been left behind by the retreating Axis forces.

To amuse himself, Ian had followed the trail of some ants for over half a mile without actually finding the nest, then saw a large dung beetle pushing its ball of dung along, making a surprising amount of noise in the process. Always interested in birds, Ian next followed some "exquisite birds for miles, real tropical types, the shine on their feathers was blinding". He then mentions that the unit has become an informal dispensary for the local nomadic tribes and that a little girl with a 'messy finger' had moved on, but that it seemed like blood poisoning so her chances of survival would be remote. Instead, there was:

"a small boy with a hole in his head. Quite a nice kid, large brown eyes, black hair. We amuse him with the mirror while we dress his mess. Never seen himself before I should think as there is no water to look into and they only drink goat and camels' milk."

However, Ian discovered there were also some quite interesting characters in the camp:

> "... quite an amusing, vague type, with very long pale yellow hair, a long drooping moustache, pale skin, long face, very 'affected', bates everyone. I don't blame him. He is interested in the stage, painting, so I am able to talk to someone about other things than cars or what so and so did on such a hill when so and so met someone who knew a WAAF etc etc. It drives me to distraction. In fact I like the people who have got a touch of the sun, they do make me laugh and are genuine but a bit pathetic. Yellow whiskers has made some shortbread but it is pretty grim – too much marge I think. He knows all about Torquay, been to all the wrong places. Unfortunately the poor bloke wants to be an interior decorator, so I am trying to help him as much as I can but he can't draw for toffee."

Vegetable garden at Garian. [Ian Baker]

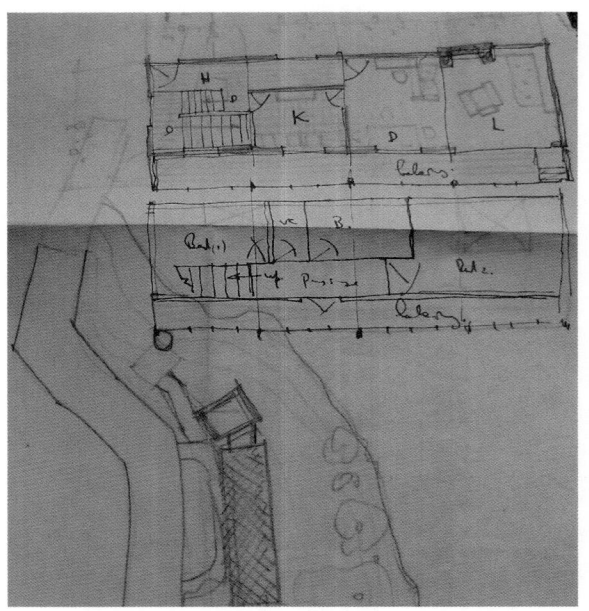 

These seem to be drawings prepared for sending to the AA School, apparently of a small sanatorium. Ian had had a much-delayed letter from the Architectural Association School asking him to submit any work he might have done whilst overseas, so evidently the school made considerable efforts to stay in touch with its students during their military service. He was apparently working on a design for a house and was therefore working hard to get the design finished and sent off. This may have been assigned work as he was apparently required to provide a lot of drawings, although he already had all the ideas roughed out on paper. The letter was signed off with a tip for Pat's technical drawings on how to do good lettering, followed by the report that he was now sunburnt to a brown corduroy colour – a later letter described this colour as "an Englishman dipped in cocoa and milk stout".

Beneath the Radar

At the end of April, Ian had been to Castel Benito for 3 days, to collect stores before returning to Garian. Maybe this was in connection with the RAF's confused orders to the Commanding Officer about closing/reopening the GEE chain, as the letter goes on to confirm that what had been rumour had been:

> "confirmed as 'pukka' by the CO, that we have been asked how long it will take to get back on the air, so it looks as though you can rely on this address for at least 3 months. It will take a month to get moving, about 2 months to get working properly, as at least half the bods have been posted or gone home for demob."

Ian seemed pretty content to remain at Garian for the rest of the time until his demob number would come round, as it was the most comfortable place he had been, although his colleague known as OAG was starting to irritate him.

The short visit to Castel Benito enabled the eating of ice creams and good meals, but the down side was that it was much hotter and dustier than at Garian, so he was glad to get back. Ian asked the Education Officer about getting drawing instruments and paper for his architectural work, but was told none was to be had except at official art classes which were being held at least a hundred miles away. Instead, Ian made himself a set of drawing compasses and raided the camp stationery store for paper and pencils.

In other good news, Ian had been able to move to a better room at Garian, where he was:

"living like a king, with two other blokes. We have our own balcony overlooking the Square, our own wash basin, desks, cupboards, carpets, clothes stand and 100 watt light bulbs. Large expanses of wall to paint on, bags of room and good beds."

Living was indeed so 'soft' that he feared he was getting fat, as he noticed that he 'wobbled', perhaps due to all the eggs and spaghetti he had been eating. In fact my father remained bean-pole thin up into his late 40s, although he always loved food and became an enthusiastic cook.

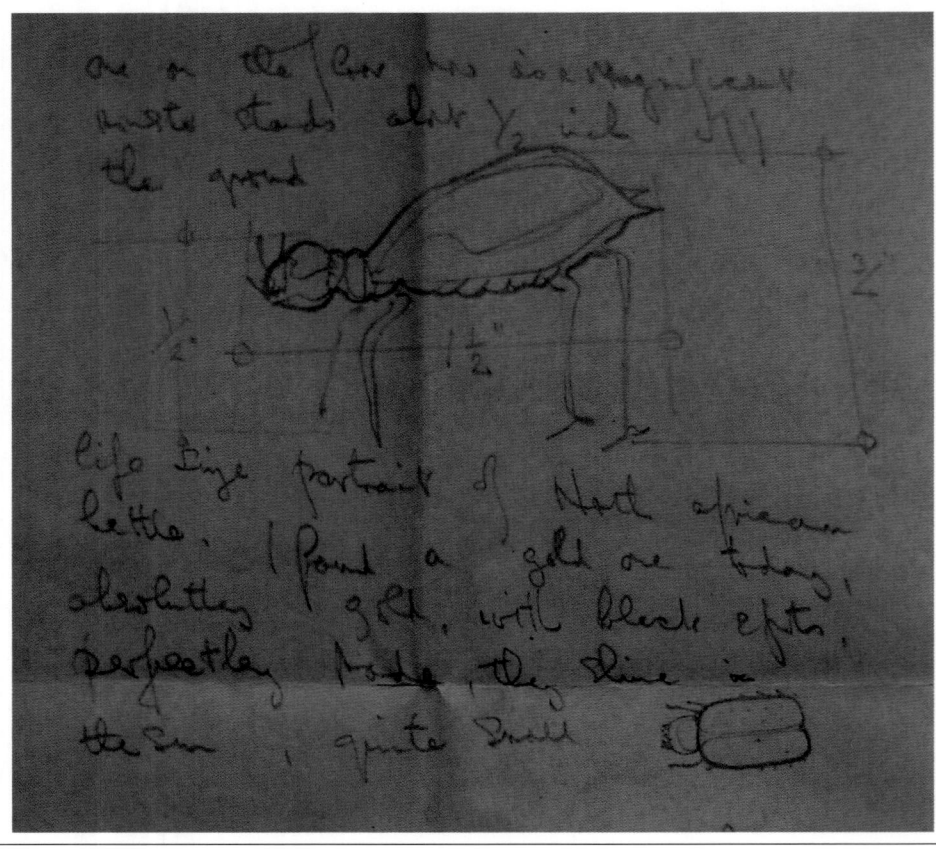

This letter also features drawings of the huge beetles which were scrabbling about in the billet, apparently making a lot of noise. Another beetle had the appearance of metallic gold, with black spots. After that letter of 30th April there is then a very long gap from which no letters remain, with the next in the collection being from 25th July. Although Ian was probably bored and hot, it seems that my future mum, Pat, was also not in a good way, apparently at a low point in both her physical and mental health, and he was trying to console her. However, he was also being uncharacteristically bad tempered with 'unbearable' colleagues, a state hard for me to even imagine as I can scarcely recall him ever being like that in later years. They expected to leave Garian on Wednesday 31st July and then be at Castel Benito for at least a month.

August 4th 1946, 141 AMES was at Castel Benito and Ian was expecting a posting, perhaps hoping for demobilisation, but there was no news on that front yet. They were fairly comfortable, albeit living in tents, and with plenty of sport, cinema and reading available to occupy them. He was not able to continue with his 'work', i.e., his architectural drawings for the AA School, as all his equipment was packed away, perhaps with a view to an imminent posting. The heat and the wait for postings and demob was getting on everyone's nerves with his colleagues arguing amongst themselves. Morale sounds low in this letter. Some 'bods' whom he did like were many tents away in what must have been a large encampment by this time.

A month later (6th September 1946) he was still there, but his long-time colleague OAG, who had been driving him mad, had just left to go back to the UK, so Ian felt on more of an even keel, despite the only other occupant of the tent being a Scotsman "so ignorant I can tolerate him". However, there was at last news of the next posting, which would be the first step on the route home.

View of El Karak & the Dead Sea
Trans Jordan from the RAF
AMES Site 1946.

The road to demob

The long-awaited posting was to AMES 21021 Madalena in Malta, about which many rumours circulated of terrible food and boredom, but also of a shopping paradise, but one sure thing would be water-rationing. Meanwhile the only work found for the RAF personnel at Castel Benito awaiting such postings had been 'fatigues' which Ian had somehow managed to mostly avoid. One way to keep cooler was to go to the cinema a lot and perhaps surprisingly, Ian liked to "get into a mass of tightly-packed people, all chattering, making most films vastly more entertaining than they originally were, not just the usual vulgar things, but very witty."

The next letter, undated but presumably only a few days later, was from Malta, where Ian had arrived the night before after a short flight from Castel Benito. Although he had not yet had time to get to see anything much, he reported that things seemed quite comfortable. The AMES station was 8 miles west of Valletta, "right on the sea, with perfect bathing. Work is on top of a hill a mile or so away. Some sort of shipping thing, like Kingswear's 272." This is the only mention in any of the letters of the specifics of the radar equipment Ian worked on or had worked on. Since my parents first met when they were both stationed at Kingswear this reference obviously had sentimental significance for them. The 272 type radar[39] was a naval radar adapted for coastal defence use as "Chain Home Extra Low".

---

[39] https://en.wikipedia.org/wiki/Type_271_radar#Coast_Defense which is largely based on Cochrane, C. Alec (2016). "Development of Naval Warning and Tactical Radar". In Kingsley, Fred (ed.). The Development of Radar Equipments for the Royal Navy, 1935-45. Springer. pp. 184-275.

Radar aerials at Malta
[Ian Baker]

Technically this was one of the earliest of the microwave-frequency radars with a very good definition at the sea surface, and became known also as the AMES Type 52. The entire system was very compact, having originally been designed to fit on destroyers, such that the operator's cabin could be mounted on a gun carriage or similar trailer, and the 'cheese segment' type antennas mounted directly on the cabin, rotating with it. Various versions of these had been used in coastal defences, always on hills, as at this site on Malta, for maximum benefit of elevation.

Their camp itself was:

> "... small, 4 stone buildings, bags of air and windows, good food and decent beds. The heat is about the same as at Tripoli except for a sea breeze which makes things quite comfortable. However, there are 2 snags. First the water is very short and it is highly chlorinated. At first it tastes vile but they say you get used to it. And the second is that you cannot send any parcels home except personal belongings, as all goods on the island are British Exports.
>
> The Customs are pretty hot too, when we came in the man asked some perfectly ridiculous questions about your camera and my drawing board, but I have still got them. All this is bloody annoying as they say there is some pretty good stuff here, but there is also no airmail parcel scheme here and the letters are not as frequent as in Tripoli."

The trucks and aerials at Malta. [Ian Baker]

Less positively, Ian had not got off to a good start on Malta as he had been put in a room with a flight sergeant with whom he had had a row in Garian. Fortunately, he was able to wangle a move to another room and on the whole the other people at the unit seemed reasonable. Amazingly, Ian (only just 23 at the time) and his long-time colleague OAG were considered to be 'old sweats' by the even younger RAF men on the site, but the best aspect of this posting was that all fatigues, cooking, and driving were done by a Maltese man attached to the unit, so that all the RAF personnel had to do was operate the actual radar, and seemingly not even very much of that either. Hence, Ian was able to take a first trip into Valletta.

The very last of the package of letters, dated 14th September, was from RAF Luca. Considering that only a few days before, in the previous letter, Ian was fully expecting to be still at the Madalena site well on into the winter months, it is clear that things were at last moving more swiftly, AMES 21021 having abruptly ceased to exist. However, mail of course would not keep up with all these movements and even the system at RAF Luca seemed not to know where Ian was meant to be: no one knew nor seemed to care. Just before he was due to fly, on Monday 17th September, a package from Pat caught up with Ian, containing a note and some chocolates. The flight would be from Malta "non-stop to Geneva, get one night's really good sleep and then on to Italy".

And with that, the letters stop and there is no direct evidence of what happened next in Ian's RAF service, but he was recorded as being transferred from Malta to "HQ" on 22nd September 1946 and his 'effective date of release' or demob was 25th October 1946, so presumably a lot of hanging around in RAF base barracks until the great day. He was eventually released from his Reserves obligations in 1952. From his promotion in December 1944 until the end of his service he never rose above the rank of Leading Aircraftman.

The RAF Demobilisation Centre was at Uxbridge, where airmen presented their Record & Release Book, which consisted of series of pages to be torn out at each stage – pay, records etc – until what remained in the book was the airman's record of service and identity card. There would have been another medical, similar to the one on entry to the service and then information from the Ministry of Labour. The final stage was the selection of a complete outfit of civilian clothing. Unlike the other services, the RAF system was entirely self-service, with each man entitled to a suit (3 styles and a wide range of fabric patterns), tie, raincoat, hat, shirt, shoes, 2 collars (and studs!) and 2 pairs of socks.

If Ian felt he had been kept in the dark for a long time about when and where he would be demobbed, he was far from the only RAF airman to feel that way – there was a lot of ill-feeling amongst them that the Army and Navy were being released quicker, but the politicians were debating the need for a larger peacetime RAF than previously, plus the RAF was needed to fly the soldiers and sailors home from all over the British Empire, as it still considered itself to be. In March 1946 it was announced that 742,000 of the RAF's strength of 1,100,000 would be released from the Service by 30 June 1946.

The first groups in each service to be demobilised were those who had been in the longest, in many cases men who had served since the First World War, so it is not surprising that Ian – born in 1923 and therefore too young to even be called up until part-way into the Second World War – would find himself waiting so long. So, with a new suit, a few quid and a travel warrant, Ian returned to the civilian world and for the first time in his life, what with the 'cocoons' of boarding schools and the RAF, the adult problems of making one's own decisions.

Prelude to another life

Returning to war-ravaged London, my father shared 'digs' of varying qualities of squalor whilst completing his studies at the Architectural Association School, graduating in 1949. He married Pat, my mother, in 1948, so an income soon became essential. Initially he did all kinds of freelance graphic design, including 'Architypes' - a set of humorous cartoon caricatures of well-known figures in architecture, planning and construction, for a series of adverts. He also did some illustrations for book covers, in a style influenced by Piper, Bawden and Ravillious.

My parents lived first in a shared flat in Brompton Road in the Kensington area and later on a converted barge at Cheyney Walk in Chelsea. In 1950 he first joined forces with Leonard Manasseh with whom he would set up their very successful architectural partnership in 1953. You can read more about their work in the RIBA book that triggered my discoveries mentioned at the start of this story, Leonard Manasseh & Partners, by Timothy Brittain-Catlin.

Acknowledgements

Although this book is heavily based on family archives, I have also had to reach out for technical advice. I would especially like to thank the experts at the Bawdsey Radar Trust museum and archives who have been a tremendous help, in particular Dr Phil Judkins for clarifying various equipment models. Squadron Leader Mike Dean MBE kindly shared items from his extensive personal collection of war diaries.

Bibliography

There are of course a lot of books about the history of radar. Here are some that I found useful:

- Building Radar. Forging Britain's early-warning chain 1935-1945. Colin Dobinson. Methuen. 2010 [For detailed history of the radar sites and development.]
- Radar Origins Worldwide. History of its evolution in 13 nations through world war II. Raymond C Watson Jr. Trafford Publishing. 2009
- Radar. A wartime miracle. Colin Latham & Anne Stobbs. Sutton Publishing Ltd. 1997 [For reminiscences of those who used radar and for the best explanation of GEE.]
- Pioneers of radar. Colin Latham & Anne Stobbs. Sutton Publishing Ltd. 1999.
- One-Oh-Eight Miller. Anne Stobbs. Bucks Literary Services. 1989. [Personal reminiscence, largely social, of her time as a radar operator.]
- The Eyes of the Few. Daphne Carne. P.R. Macmillan Ltd. 1960 [Personal reminiscence of her time as a radar operator, with a good deal more about the work than other similar WAAF memoirs.]
- Reflexions on a chain of events. Ray Barker. Janus 1992. [Personal reminiscence of his time as a radar operator, in UK and Europe.]

Printed in Great Britain
by Amazon